2008
CHINA

FOREIGN LANGUAGES PRESS

General Planning: Zhou Mingwei

Chief Editors: Zhou Mingwei, Huang Youyi, Guo Changjian, Wu Wei

Executive Chief Editors: Xu Mingqiang, Hu Baomin

Deputy Chief Editors: Li Zhenguo, Chen Shi

English Editors: May Yee, Wang Mingjie

English Translators: Li Yang, Yan Jing, Qu Lei, Wang Qin,
 Zhou Xiaogang, Li Lei, Han Qingyue, Feng Xin

Title page seal by Luo Pengpeng

First Edition 2008

ISBN 978-7-119-05207-6

© Foreign Languages Press, Beijing, China, 2008

Published by Foreign Languages Press

24 Baiwanzhuang Road, Beijing 100037, China

http://www.flp.com.cn

Designed by Beijing Great Union Culture and Art Co., Ltd.

Printed by C&C Joint Printing Co., (Beijing) Ltd.

Distributed by China International Book Trading Corporation

35 Chegongzhuang Xilu, Beijing 100044, China

P.O. Box 399, Beijing, China

Printed in the People's Republic of China

Foreword

Whenever China is brought up, people often think of its long-standing history and brilliant culture including the Great Wall, the Terracotta Warriors, the Forbidden City, along with other famous cultural and natural landscapes and ancient treasures coming to mind.

Since adoption of reform and opening-up in 1978, China's economy has maintained steady rapid development, accompanied by remarkable social changes. People have begun to pay increasing attention not only to its ancient civilization, but to China's vibrant present and future.

Since 1992, every year we have published the China yearbook, to give a general overview on the country, and provide readers with up-to-date information on China's current conditions and changes, in terms of politics, economy, culture, etc.

China 2008 is a primer to help foreign readers acquire a better understanding of China, including extensive updates on the country's development and changes since 2007, while maintaining certain basic historical facts and general information. It offers the latest facts and figures on every facet of China, including its international contacts, cultural exchanges, economic growth, environmental protection, developments in science and technology, social progress, and improvement of people's livelihood, with the aim of assisting readers toward a wider and deeper knowledge of China.

We hope you will find this book useful.

CONTENTS

◤ Population and Ethnicity

◤ Political System and State Structure

◤ China and the World

The Economy

Environmental Protection

Location of the People's Republic of China

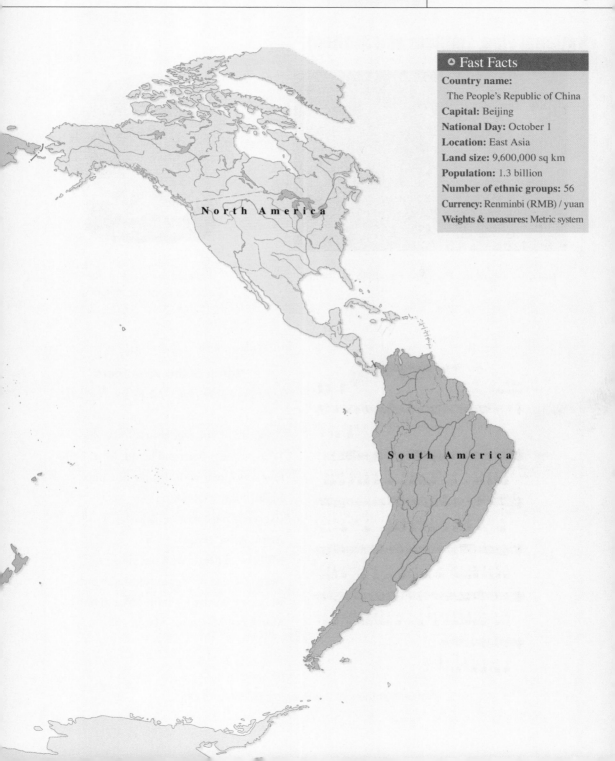

North America

South America

⊙ Fast Facts

Country name:
The People's Republic of China
Capital: Beijing
National Day: October 1
Location: East Asia
Land size: 9,600,000 sq km
Population: 1.3 billion
Number of ethnic groups: 56
Currency: Renminbi (RMB) / yuan
Weights & measures: Metric system

National Flag, Emblem and Anthem

National flag of the People's Republic of China

National emblem of the
People's Republic of China

"March of the Volunteers"

Lyrics by: Tian Han   Music by: Nie Er

Arise, all of you who refuse to be slaves –
With our very flesh and blood, let us build
Our new Great Wall! People of China:
In this most vital hour,
Everyone must roar defiance!
Arise! Arise! Arise!
Millions of hearts with one resolve:
Brave the enemy's gunfire! March on!
Brave the enemy's gunfire! March on!
March on! March on, March on!

National anthem of the People's Republic of China

State Leaders

Hu Jintao

President of the People's Republic
of China

Wu Bangguo

Chairman of the Standing
Committee of the National
People's Congress

Wen Jiabao

Premier of the State Council

Jia Qinglin

Chairman of the Chinese
People's Political Consultative
Conference

Land and Resources

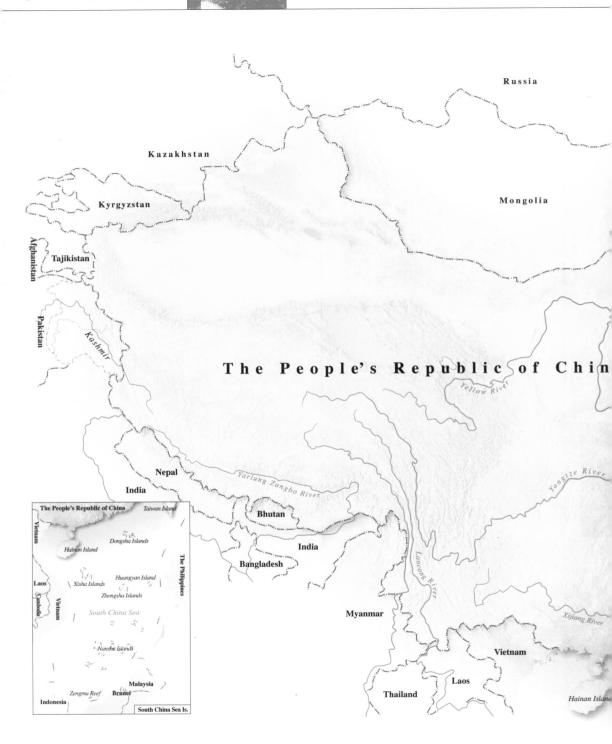

Russia

Kazakhstan

Mongolia

Kyrgyzstan

Afghanistan

Tajikistan

Pakistan

Kashmir

The People's Republic of Chin

Yellow River

Nepal

India

Yarlung Zangbo River

Yangtze River

Bhutan

India

Bangladesh

Lancang River

Myanmar

Xijiang River

Vietnam

Laos

Thailand

Hainan Island

Inset map:

The People's Republic of China   Taiwan Island

Vietnam

Hainan Island

Dongsha Islands

The Philippines

Laos

Cambodia

Vietnam

Huangyan Island

Xisha Islands

Zhongsha Islands

South China Sea

Nansha Islands

Malaysia

Zengmu Reef   Brunei

Indonesia

South China Sea Is.

Beijing ★

Bohai Sea

D.P.R. Korea

R.O. Korea

Japan

Yellow Sea

East China Sea

Chiwei Island

Diaoyu Island

Taiwan Island

Penghu Islands

Dongsha Islands

South China Sea

The Philippines

Heilong River

Xingkai Lake

Yellow River

Yangtze River

Taiwan Straits

Land Area

Located in the eastern part of the Asian continent, on the western shore of the Pacific, the People's Republic of China has a land area of 9.6 million sq km, and is the third largest country in the world, next only to Russia and Canada. From north to south, the territory of China stretches from the center of the Heilong River north of the town of Mohe to the Zengmu Reef at the southernmost tip of the Nansha Islands, covering a length of 5,500 km. From east to west, the country extends from the confluence of the Heilong and Wusuli rivers to the Pamir Mountains, spanning a width of 5,200 km.

China's mainland coastline measures approximately 18,000 km, with a flat topography, and many excellent harbors, most of which are ice-free all year round. The Chinese mainland is flanked to the east and south by the Bohai, Yellow, East China and South China seas, with a total maritime area of 4.73 million sq km. The Bohai Sea is China's continental sea, while the Yellow, East China and South China seas are marginal seas of the Pacific.

Islands

A total of 5,400 islands dot China's territorial waters. The largest of these, with an area of about 36,000 sq km, is Taiwan, followed by Hainan with an area of 34,000 sq km. The Diaoyu and Chiwei islands, located to the northeast of Taiwan Island, are China's easternmost islands. The many islands, islets, reefs and shoals in the South China Sea, known collectively as the South China Sea Islands, are China's southernmost island group. They are called the Dongsha Islands, Xisha Islands, Zhongsha Islands and Nansha Islands, according to their geographical locations.

Neighboring Countries

With land boundaries totaling about 22,800 km, China is bordered by the Democratic People's Republic of Korea (DPRK) to the east; Mongolia to the north; Russia to the northeast; Kazakhstan, Kyrgyzstan and Tajikistan to the northwest; Afghanistan, Pakistan, India, Nepal and Bhutan to the west and southwest; and Myanmar, Laos and Vietnam to the south. Across the seas to the east and southeast are the Republic of Korea (ROK), Japan, the Philippines, Brunei, Malaysia and Indonesia.

Mountain Ranges

China has at least nine mountain ranges with an average elevation of 6,000 m and above, and over 20 ranges with an average elevation of 4,000 and above. The Himalayas, the highest mountain range, extending over the border of China with India, Nepal and other countries, contains over 30 peaks of 7,300 m or higher above sea level and 11 peaks of 8,000 m or higher in elevation. Soaring 8,844.43 m above sea level is Mount Qomolangma, the world's highest peak and the main peak of the Himalayas. The Kunlun mountain range, averaging 5,500 m to 6,000 m in elevation, spans from west to east over Xinjiang, Tibet, Qinghai and Sichuan. Measuring 2,500 km long and 200 to 500 km wide, the Kunlun is the longest range in China. The Thanglha and Qinling mountains are also notable. The Thanglha in the central Qinghai-Tibet Plateau, averaging 6,000 m above sea level, is the source of the Yangtze, China's longest river. The Qinling Mountains, extending west to east from eastern Gansu Province to western Henan Province, with average elevations of 2,000 m to 3,000 m, make up a geographical division line for northern and southern China's differing culture and climate.

Plateaus

China has four major plateaus. The Qinghai-Tibet Plateau, consisting of all of Qinghai and Tibet and parts of Gansu, Yunnan and Sichuan, is the world's highest plateau. Averaging 4,000 m above sea level, the Qinghai-Tibet Plateau is considered the "roof of the world." The Inner Mongolia Plateau in Inner Mongolia is flanked by grasslands in the east and desert in the west. The Loess Plateau, comprising all or parts of six provinces and autonomous regions, including Shaanxi and Shanxi, is thickly covered by loess and suffers from serious water and soil loss. The Yunnan-Guizhou Plateau, composed of eastern Yunnan Province and most of Guizhou Province, has typical karstic topography.

Plains

China's three largest plains are in sequence, the Northeast Plain of more than 350,000 sq km, the North China Plain of about 300,000 sq km in central China, and the Middle-Lower Yangtze Plain of around 200,000 sq km with a low,

flat terrain and an elevation below 50 m, formed by alluvial of the Yangtze River.

The Topography of China

- Plateau
- Plain
- Basin
- Hill
- Mountain

Mount Qomolangma

Qinghai-Tibet Plateau

Basins

China has four major basins. The Tarim Basin in the Xinjiang Uyghur Autonomous Region is China's largest basin and contains China's largest and the world's second largest desert, the Taklimakan Desert. The Junggar Basin is located in the same region. The Qaidam Basin in Qinghai Province is the highest basin in China. The Sichuan Basin in Sichuan Province is China's wettest basin.

Grand Canyon of Yarlung Zangbo

Rivers

China abounds in rivers. More than 1,500 rivers each drain 1,000 sq km or larger areas. As a result, China is rich in waterpower resources, leading the world in hydropower potential, with reserves of 680 million kw. Due to its large population, however, China's per-capita volume of water resources takes up only one quarter of the world's average.

China's rivers can be categorized as exterior and interior systems. The catchment area of the exterior rivers that empty into the oceans accounts for 64 percent of the country's total land area. The catchment area of the interior rivers that flow into inland lakes or disappear into deserts or salt marshes makes up about 36 percent of China's total land area.

The Yangtze, 6,300 km long, is the longest river in China, and the third longest in the world. Passing through high mountains and deep valleys, the upper section of the Yangtze River is abundant in water resources. The Yangtze is a transportation artery linking west and east, its navigation benefiting from excellent natural channels. The Yellow River is the second longest river in China, with a length of 5,464 km. The Yellow River valley is one of the birthplaces of ancient Chinese civilization. The Heilong River is a major river in northeastern China, with a total length of 4,350 km, of which 3,101 km go through China. The Pearl River, 2,214 km long, is a major river in southern China. In southern Xinjiang the Tarim River's 2,179 km make it China's longest interior river.

In addition to those bestowed by nature, China has a famous manmade waterway — the Grand Canal, running from Beijing in the north to Zhejiang Province's Hangzhou in the south. Work began on the Grand Canal as early as in the fifth century BC. It links five major rivers: the Haihe, Yellow, Huaihe, Yangtze and Qiantang. With a total length of 1,801 km, the Grand Canal is the longest as well as the oldest artificial waterway in the world.

Lakes

China's territory includes numerous lakes. Most of those lakes are found on the Middle-Lower Reaches of Yangtze Plain and the Qinghai-Tibet Plateau. Freshwater lakes such as Poyang, Dongting, Taihu and Hongze mostly lie in the former area, while in the latter are found saltwater lakes, such as Qinghai, Nam Co, and Serling Co. Poyang Lake, in northern

Jiangxi Province and with an area of 3,583 sq km, making it the largest of its kind. Northeast Qinghai Province's Qinghai Lake, with an area of 4,583 sq km, is the largest saltwater lake.

South China Sea Is.

- Water-rich zone
- Water-sufficient zone
- Transitional zone
- Water-deficient zone
- Water-scarce zone

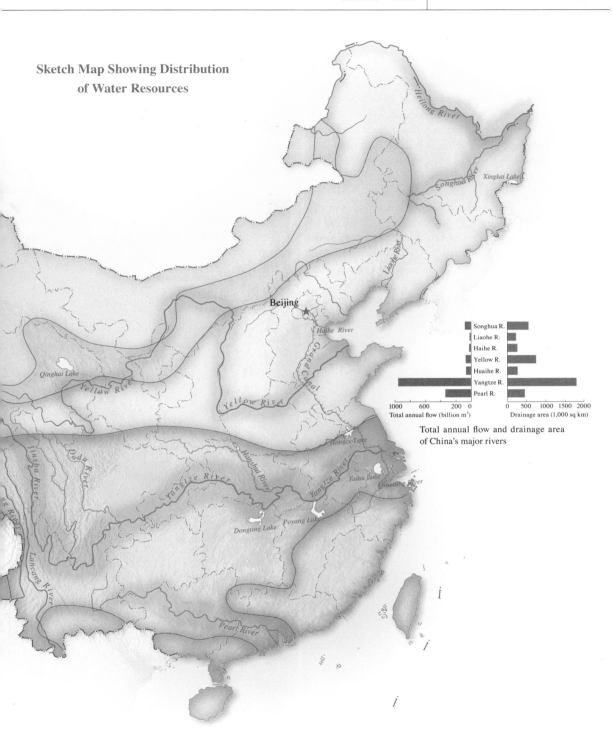

**Sketch Map Showing Distribution
of Water Resources**

Total annual flow and drainage area
of China's major rivers

Climate

Most of China lies in the northern temperate zone, characterized by distinctive seasons and a continental monsoon climate, which is well suited for habitation. From September to April of the following year, the dry and cold winter monsoons blow from Siberia and the Mongolian Plateau, resulting in cold and dry winters and great differences between the temperatures of northern and southern China. From April to September, warm and humid summer monsoons blow from the seas in the east and south, resulting in overall high temperatures and abundant rainfall, and little temperature difference between northern and southern China. In terms of temperature, the country can be sectored from south to north into equatorial, tropical, subtropical, warm-temperate, temperate, and cold-temperate zones. Precipitation gradually declines from the southeastern coast to the northwestern inlands, with the average annual precipitation varying greatly from place to place. In the southeastern coastal areas, it is over 1,500 mm; while in northwestern areas, it drops to below 200 mm.

Snow scenery of Northeast China

Tropical landscape of Hainan Island

Sketch Map Showing Rainfall Distribution

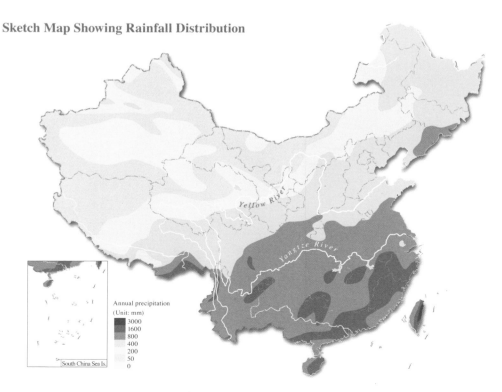

Yellow River

Yangtze River

Annual precipitation
(Unit: mm)
3000
1600
800
400
200
50
0

South China Sea Is.

Sketch Map Showing Climate Categories

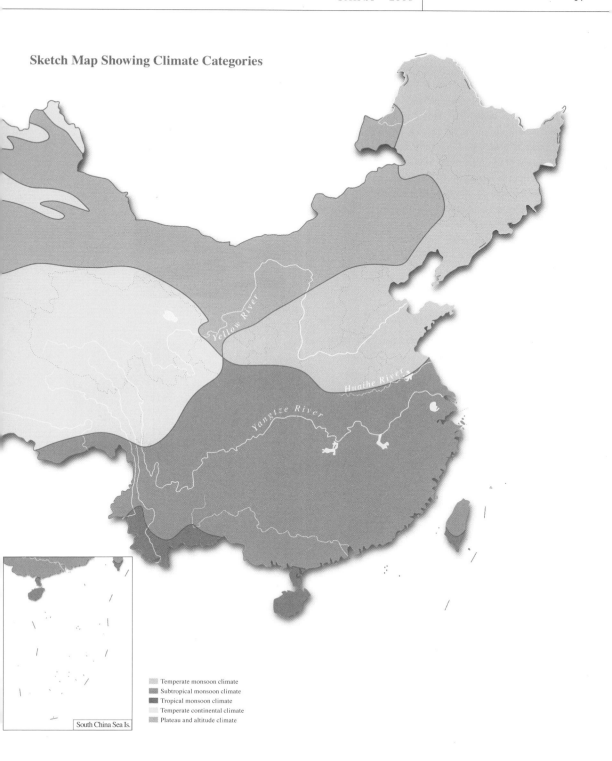

Yellow River

Huaihe River

Yangtze River

Temperate monsoon climate
Subtropical monsoon climate
Tropical monsoon climate
Temperate continental climate
Plateau and altitude climate

South China Sea Is.

Land

Cultivated land, forests, grasslands, deserts and tidelands are distributed widely across China. Cultivated land is mainly located in eastern China; grasslands are mainly located in the north and the west, and forests mainly in the remote northeastern and southwestern areas. In China today, 121.78 million ha of land are cultivated; grasslands cover an area of 400 million ha, or 41.6 percent of China's total land size; forests cover 174.91 million ha, with the forest coverage rate rising to 18.21 percent. China's cultivated lands, forests and grasslands are among the world's largest in terms of sheer area. But due to China's large population, the per-capita areas of cultivated land, forest and grassland are small, especially in the case of cultivated land, which is only one third of the world average.

Chessboard-like farmland

Terraced fields in southwestern China

Sketch Map Showing Forest and Pasture Areas

Sketch Map Showing Agricultural Areas

Natural Forests

The Greater Hinggan, Lesser Hinggan and Changbai mountain ranges in the northeast are China's largest natural forest areas. Major tree species found here include conifers and broadleaf trees. Major tree species in the southwest include dragon spruce, fir and Yunnan pine. Often called a "kingdom of plants," Xishuangbanna in the south of Yunnan Province is a rare tropical broadleaf forest area in China, playing host to more than 5,000 plant species.

Cultivated Lands

China's cultivated lands are mainly located on the Northeast Plain, the North China Plain, the Middle-Lower Reaches of Yangtze Plain, the Pearl River Delta, and the Sichuan Basin. The Northeast Plain abounds in wheat, corn, soybean, sorghum, flax, and sugar beet. The North China Plain is planted with wheat, corn, millet, and cotton. The Middle-Lower Reaches of Yangtze Plain's low, flat terrain and many lakes and rivers make it particularly suitable for paddy rice and freshwater fish, hence its designation as "land of fish and rice." This area also produces large quantities of tea and silkworms. The Sichuan Basin in all four seasons is green with crops, including paddy rice, rapeseed and sugarcane, making it known as the "land of plenty." The Pearl River Delta abounds with paddy rice, harvested twice to three times every year.

Natural Pasturelands

Grasslands in China stretch several thousand kilometers from the northeast to the southwest, including quite a few centers of animal husbandry. The Inner Mongolian Prairie is China's largest natural pastureland, and home to the legendary Sanhe horses, Sanhe cattle and Mongolian sheep. The important natural pasturelands north and south of the Tianshan Mountains in Xinjiang are ideal for stockbreeding. Famed Ili horses and Xinjiang fine-wool sheep are raised here.

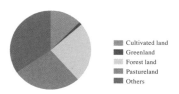

- Cultivated land
- Greenland
- Forest land
- Pastureland
- Others

Mineral Resources

China is rich in mineral resources, and all the world's known minerals can be found here. To date, geologists have confirmed reserves of 158 kinds of minerals, putting China third in the world in terms of total reserves. Reserves of major mineral resources, such as coal, iron, copper, aluminum, stibium, molybdenum, manganese, tin, lead, zinc and mercury, are front-ranking in the world. China's basic coal reserves total 333.5 billion tons, mainly distributed in northwestern and northern China, with Shanxi, Shaanxi, Xinjiang and Inner Mongolia heading the field. China's 22.1 billion tons of basic iron ore reserves are mainly distributed in the northeast, north and southwest. The national reserves of rare earth metal far exceed the combined total of the rest of the world.

The country also abounds in petroleum, natural gas and oil shale. Petroleum reserves are mainly found in northwest China, as well as in northeast and northern China and the continental shelves of eastern China.

Metal deposits and reserves			
▲ Iron 22.09 b. tons	⊗ Lead 13.514 m. tons	Ⓥ Vanadium 14.044 m. tons	⊘ Molybdenum 3.81 m. tons
⊷ Manganese 229 m. tons	⬗ Tin 1.535 m. tons	▬ Copper 30.699 m. tons	△ Aluminum 740 m. tons
△ Nickel 2.727 m. tons	◑ Gold 1,995 tons	⊗ Silver 45,000 tons	▣ Antimony 0.95 m. tons
Ⓦ Tungsten 2.414 m. tons	◪ Chromium 5.214 m. tons	▲ Rare earth 19.059 m. tons	◍ Lithium
⌂ Mercury	◻ Magnesium	◤ Uranium	⊕ Titanium

Nonmetal deposits and reserves		
◆ Magnesite 1.9 b. tons	◮ Salt mines 183.3 b. tons	■ Coal 333.48 b. tons
△ Sylvite 270 m. tons	● Phosphorite 3.7 b. tons	▌ Petroleum 2.76 b. tons
◈ Fluorite 34.774 m. tons	▲ Sulfur	◻ Natural gas 3000.92 b. m³
◖ Mica	▣ Asbestos	
◇ Boron	✷ Diamond	

Pinghu Oil and Gas Field on East China Sea

Huaibei Coal Mine in Anhui

South China Sea Is.

Sketch Map Showing Distribution
of Mineral Resources

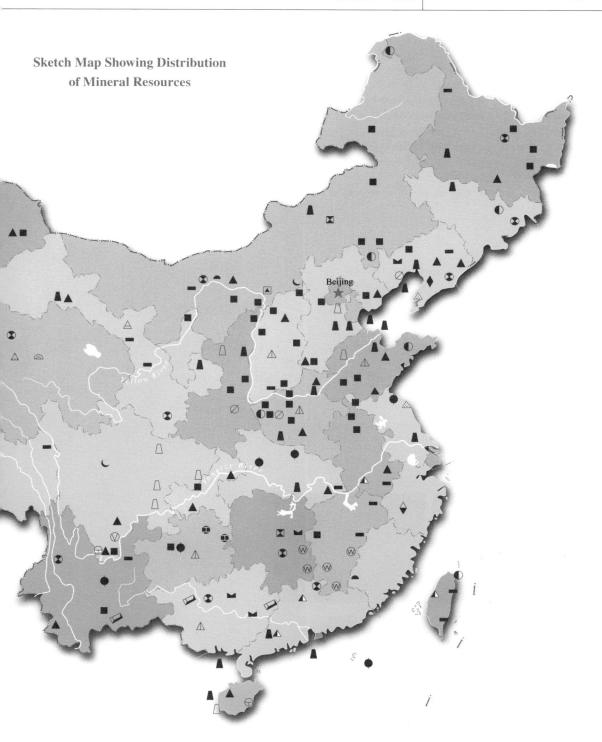

Plants and Animals

China is one of the countries with the greatest diversity of wildlife in the world. There are more than 6,266 species of vertebrates, 10% of the world's total. Among them, 2,404 are terrestrial and 3,862 marine life. China boasts more than 32,000 species of higher plants, among which are more than 7,000 species of woody plants, including 2,800-odd tree species, over 2,000 species of edible plants, and 3,000 or more species of medicinal plants. Almost all the major plants that grow in the northern hemisphere's frigid, temperate and tropical zones are to be found in China.

Unique Species

There are more than 100 wild animal species unique to China including such well-known rare animals as the giant panda, golden-haired monkey, South China tiger, brown-eared pheasant, red-crowned crane, crested ibis, white-flag dolphin, and Chinese alligator. The metasequoia, Chinese cypress, Cathay silver fir, China fir, golden larch, Taiwan fir, Fujian cypress, dove-tree, eucommia and camplotheca acuminata are tree species found only in China. The metasequoia, a tall species of arbor, is one of the oldest and rarest plants in the world. The golden larch, one of only five species of rare garden trees in the world, grows in the mountainous areas in the Yangtze River valley. Its coin-shaped leaves on short branches are green in spring and summer, turning yellow in autumn.

Crested ibis

Dove tree

Kingdonia uniflora Balf

China fir

Sketch Map Showing Distribution of Rare Animals and Different Vegetation

Reindeer

I

Wolverine   Moose

Musk Deer   Sable

Swan   Northeast China Tiger

Red-crowned Crane   II

Bustard   Mandarin Duck

Mongolian Gazelle   VIII   Spotted Deer

orse

ild Donkey   Blue Sheep

Bustard   Mongolian Gazelle   Swan

Stoat

Stone Marten   Macaque

ed Gazelle   Goitered Gazelle   Long-tailed Pheasant

Brown-eared Pheasant

Bharal   IX

Black-necked Crane   Giant Salamander   III

Argali   Macaque   Swan

White-lipped Deer   White-eared Pheasant   Blue Sheep

Golden Monkey   Roe Deer

Giant Panda   Roe Deer   Musk Deer

Musk Deer   Spotted Deer   Spotted Deer   White-finned Dolphin

Long-tailed Pheasant   Swan   Mandarin Duck

Tragopan   Mandarin Duck   Yangtze Crocodile

Antelope   Tufted Deer   White-finned Dolphin   Long-tailed Pheasant   Macaque

V   IV   Black Muntjac

Red Panda   Macaque   Tufted Deer

Golden Monkey   Golden Monkey

Giant Salamander   Tragopan

Buffalo   Taiwan Monkey

Loris   Crocodile Lizard   Spotted Deer   Musk Deer   VI

Peacock   Langur Monkey   Black Gibbon

Great Hornbill   Wild Elephant   VII   Long-tailed Pheasant

VI

South China Tiger

Black Gibbon   VI

Hainan Eld's Deer

I   Zone of cold temperate coniferous forests
II   Zone of mixed temperate coniferous and deciduous broadleaf forests
III   Zone of warm temperate deciduous broadleaf forests
IV   Zone of eastern subtropical evergreen broadleaf forests
V   Zone of western subtropical evergreen broadleaf forests
VI   Zone of eastern tropical rainforests and rainforests
VII   Zone of western tropical rainforests and rainforests
VIII   Zone of temperate grasslands
IX   Zone of warm temperate grasslands
X   Zone of alpine meadow and grasslands
XI   Zone of temperate deserts
XII   Zone of warm temperate deserts
XIII   Zone of alpine deserts

History

Ancient Civilization

China, one of the world's most ancient civilizations, has a recorded history of nearly 4,000 years. Cultivated rice and millet as well as farming tools have been found in the Hemudu remains in Yuyao, Zhejiang Province, and Banpo remains, near Xi'an in Shaanxi Province. These relics date back 6,000 to 7,000 years. The Chinese mastered the technology of smelting bronze 5,000 years ago. China's earliest society appeared over 4,000 years ago in the Xia Dynasty (2070-1600 BC). During the Shang Dynasty (1600-1046 BC), iron tools came into use. The Western Zhou (1046-221 BC) witnessed the emergence of steel production technology. During the Spring and Autumn and the Warring States periods (770-221 BC), there was a great upsurge of intellectual activity, producing many famous philosophers such as Lao Zi, Confucius (Kong Zi), Mencius (Meng Zi), Mo Zi, Han Fei Zi, as well as the well-known military strategist Sun Wu, author of the *Art of War.*

The Yin Ruins is the site of China's earliest ancient capital. The picture shows Simuwu Quadripod unearthed in the area of Yin Ruins.

Oracle Bone Inscription

In the early 20th century, archeologists discovered nearly 100,000 pieces of tortoise shells and cattle bones from the ruins of Yin, capital of the Shang Dynasty, in Anyang, Henan Province. These shells and bones are inscribed with nearly 5,000 different characters, recording various Shang activities, such as worship of ancestors and deities, wars and battles, appointment of official posts, construction of cities, and fortunetelling by divination. Oracle bone inscriptions are the earliest signs of legible Chinese written language discovered so far.

Unification and Dissemination of Civilization

In 221 BC Qin Shi Huang, or the First Emperor of Qin, put an end to the several hundred years of rivalry among independent principalities, and established the first centralized, unified, multiethnic feudal state in Chinese history — the Qin Dynasty (221-206 BC). From then onward, until 1911, China experienced altogether 13 unified feudal dynasties and two relatively stable multi-dynasty periods.

During these long years in China, the "four great inventions" — papermaking, printing, compass and gunpowder — emerged one after the other. Agriculture, handicrafts and commerce flourished and textile, dyeing, ceramic and smelting technologies were well developed. Around the first year AD, the Han Dynasty (206 BC-AD 220) pioneered the route known as the "Silk Road," from Chang'an (today's Xi'an, Shaanxi Province), through today's Xinjiang and Central Asia, and on to the eastern shores of the Mediterranean. All types of Chinese goods, including silks and porcelains, were traded

Statue of the First Emperor of the Qin Dynasty.

abroad along the Silk Road. Thereafter, the "four great inventions" and other Chinese advances in science and culture successively spread all over the world.

Within a history of nearly 300 years, the Tang Dynasty (AD 618-907) pushed the prosperity of China's feudal society to its peak. By the 660s, China's influence had firmly taken root in the Tarim and Junggar basins and the Ili River valley, even extending as far as many city-states in Central Asia. During this period, extensive economic and cultural relations were established with many countries, including Japan, Korea, India, Persia and Arab. With the boom of the ship-building industry of the Ming Dynasty (1368-1644) in the 15th century, Zheng He led a fleet of many large ships to make seven far-ranging voyages. Going through some 30 countries including Southeast Asian countries, the Indian Ocean, the Persian Gulf and the Maldives Islands, Zheng He explored as far as Somalia and Kenya on the eastern coast of Africa.

Post-17th-century Changes

During the 17th and the 18th centuries, the Qing Dynasty (1644-1911), the best known of the Qing emperors, Kangxi (r. 1661-1722) restored the central empire's rule over Taiwan, and resisted invasions by tsarist Russia. To reinforce the administration of Tibet, he also formulated the rules and regulations on the confirmation of the Tibetan local leaders by the Central Government. He effectively administered more than 11 million sq km of Chinese territory. During the early 19th century, the Qing Dynasty declined rapidly. Britain smuggled large quantities of opium into China, leading to the Qing government imposing a ban on the drug. To protect its opium trade, Britain launched a war of aggression against China in 1840, forcing the Qing government to sign the Treaty of Nanjing, a treaty of national betrayal and humiliation. Many countries, including Britain, the United States, France, Russia and Japan, coerced the Qing government to sign various unequal treaties, cede territory and pay reparations following the Opium Wars. China was gradually relegated to the status of a semi-colonial, semi-feudal country.

Dr. Sun Yat-sen

The Revolution of 1911 led by Dr. Sun Yat-sen was one of the greatest events in modern Chinese history, as it overthrew the Qing Dynasty that had ruled for some 270 years, ended over 2,000 years of feudal monarchy, and established the Republic of China.

From 1911 to 1949 China endured a large number of civil wars. Owing to the cooperation and joint resistance of the Communist Party of China (CPC) and the Kuomintang, the Japanese aggressors were defeated in the War of Resistance against Japanese Aggression (1937-45).

The People's Republic of China was founded in 1949. Through over 50 years of struggle, achievement, trial and error and reform, as the party in power, the CPC has succeeded in bringing about a stable political situation, with a burgeoning economy, providing ample food and clothing, and active diplomatic engagement as the world's most-populous developing country.

Some Key Figures in Chinese History

Yan and Huang Emperors

The legendary Yan and Huang emperors, who lived in early 26th century BC, are revered as the ancestors of the Chinese nation; hence the Chinese people refer to themselves as the "descendants of Yan and Huang."

Sima Qian

Sima Qian (c. 145-87 BC), a historiographer of the Han Dynasty, completed China's first general history, *Shi Ji (Records of the Historian)*, around 100 BC. The book records the parts of Chinese history covering the era of the legendary Emperor Huang to 122 BC, initiating a writing style of presenting history in the form of a series of biographies.

Confucius, Lao Zi and Sun Wu

The period of over 400 years, from the seventh to the third centuries BC, was the classical era in Chinese philosophy. This epoch witnessed the creation of the main bodies of Chinese philosophy, namely Confucianism, Legalism and Taoism, as well as dozens of other schools of thoughts, including Military Strategists, Mohism and the theory of the five elements. Among this array, Confucius and his *Analects*, Lao Zi and his *Classic of the Way and Virtue*, and Sun Wu and his *Art of War* are the most representative of this era.

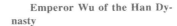

Spring & Autumn Period (770-476 BC)	Warring States Period (475-221 BC)	Qin Dynasty (221-206 BC)	Han Dynasty (206 BC-AD 220)

Qin Shi Huang

As the first emperor to unify China, Qin Shi Huang (259-210 BC)standardized the written script, weights and measures, and currency, and established the system of prefectures and counties, as well as the system of regulations and decrees. The feudal governmental structure established by him was subsequently followed for over 2,000 years. The emperor built the Great Wall, northern thoroughfare and his mausoleum, which presents a grand "underground army" of 8,000 vivid, life-sized terracotta warriors, horses and chariots.

Emperor Wu of the Han Dynasty

Liu Che (156-87 BC), or Emperor Wu of the Han Dynasty, ascended the throne at the age of 16. He solidified the centralization of power and retracted trade management rights involving salt, iron and coin foundries, putting them under the control of the government. He pushed the Han Dynasty to its apex, through launching water conservancy projects, harnessing the Yellow River, enhancing boundary defenses and extending the "Silk Road" to the western regions and Europe.

Zhang Heng

Zhang Heng (78-139), a scientist of the Han Dynasty, invented the world's first water-powered armillary sphere to measure astronomical phenomena and the first wind-driven seismograph for predicting earthquakes. In addition, he was the first to explain the formation of lunar eclipses and to reveal the relationship between the rotation speed of planets and their distance from the Earth.

Cai Lun

In 105, Cai Lun (?-121), a eunuch of the Han Dynasty, invented plant-fiber paper from bark, fishnet, rags and hemp. Such paper was well suited for writing, and its diverse raw materials brought down costs, facilitating the popularization of paper in China and around the world.

Zu Chongzhi

Zu Chongzhi (429-500), a mathematician of the Northern and Southern dynasties, was the first in the world to calculate the value of π to seven decimal places.

Jianzhen

Jianzhen (688-763), an eminent monk of the Tang Dynasty, at the age of 14 converted to study in the Lü sect (Vinaya sect) of Buddhism. In the year of 753, he was invited by a Japanese monastery to preach and disseminate the Buddhist Lü sect in Japan. At that time, he also brought advanced Chinese knowledge of architecture, sculpture, painting and medicine to Japan.

Three Kingdoms Period (220-280)	Jin Dynasty (265-420)	Southern & Northern Dynasties (420-589)	Sui Dynasty (581-618)	Tang Dynasty (618-907)

Emperor Taizong of the Tang Dynasty

Li Shimin (599-649), or Emperor Taizong of the Tang Dynasty, perfected the imperial civil examination system for selecting talent, implemented a more equal field system and initiated water conservancy projects to develop agriculture. During his reign, he also maintained the constant free flow of traffic along the "Silk Road," to promote economic and cultural exchange between the Tang Dynasty and foreign countries.

Wang Xizhi

Wang Xizhi (321-379), renowned calligrapher of the Eastern Jin Dynasty, advanced Chinese calligraphy to new heights and enjoyed the honorific title of "master of calligraphy." His enduring work, *Preface to the Orchid Pavilion Poem Collection*, is regarded as a treasure of Chinese calligraphy.

Li Bai and Du Fu

Classical Chinese poetry reached its prime during the Tang Dynasty. At that time poets emerged by the thousands, creating innumerable poems, including over 50,000 passed to the present day. Among them, the romantic poems of Li Bai (701-762) and the realistic poems of Du Fu (712-770) embody the highest level of classical Chinese poetry.

Su Shi

Su Shi (1037-1101), a man of letters and calligrapher of the Northern Song Dynasty, was famous for his fresh poetry style and unconstrained *ci* (lyrics). His consummate calligraphy was between running and cursive scripts, while his paintings excelled in fantastic rockery and withered trees.

Genghis Khan and the Ming Dynasty

Genghis Khan(1162-1227), born Temüjin, became a Mongol chieftain who unified the Mongolian grasslands with his exceptional political and military tactics and strategies; and in 1215 he took control of northern China, laying the foundation for his descendants to establish a vast, global grassland empire. In 1271 Kublai (1215-1294), the grandson of Genghis Khan, founded the unified Yuan Dynasty. Lasting nearly a hundred years, the Yuan was the first dynasty under non-Han rule in Chinese history. Tibet was included as part of the territory of Yuan Dynasty China.

Song Dynasty (960-1279)	Yuan Dynasty (1271-1368)

Bi Sheng

Bi Sheng (?-c. 1051) of the Song Dynasty invented movable-type printing. He carved individual character on clay cubes and burned them into pottery. The pottery types were arranged within an iron frame. Printing and typesetting could proceed at the same time. The pottery types could be reused repeatedly. Movable-type printing is considered a major revolution in the printing history of humankind.

Zhu Xi

Zhu Xi (1130-1200), famed philosopher of the Southern Song Dynasty, during his whole adult life presided over an academy of classical studies. He worked as a teacher for over 50 years and fostered innumerous students. His ideas on philosophy became orthodox ideologies during the Ming and Qing dynasties.

Guan Hanqing

Guan Hanqing (c. 1220-1300) was a Yuan-dynasty dramatist in the 13th century. He created more than 60 kinds of *zaju* (poetic dramas set to music, flourishing in the Yuan) during his life. His representative works are: *Snow in Midsummer*, *Butterfly Dream*, *Moon-Worshiping Pavilion*, *Single-Knife Meeting*, etc.

Kangxi

Xuanye, or Emperor Kangxi (1654-1722), ascended the throne at age 8, and by the time he was 13, began to handle state affairs independently. During his reign, he recovered Taiwan, blocked the expansion of Russia and instituted a complete set of regulations that stipulated Tibetan chieftain appointments to be determined by the central government. He also encouraged wasteland cultivation, harnessed rivers and guaranteed the free navigation of the Grand Canal.

Hong Xiuquan

Hong Xiuquan (1814-1864) initiated an uprising in 1851 and established the Taiping Heavenly Kingdom. With an aim to overthrow the Qing Dynasty, he proclaimed himself "Celestial Emperor." In 1853, the Taiping army captured Nanjing, where they settled as the capital. Hong Xiuquan died after an illness, before the uprising was ultimately suppressed.

Zheng He

Zheng He (1371-1435), a eunuch of the Ming Dynasty, was assigned to lead huge fleets to voyage the Western Seas for seven missions from 1405 to 1433. They passed through 30 countries and reached as far as the eastern coast of Africa and the Red Sea estuary.

Ming Dynasty (1368-1644)	Qing Dynasty (1644-1911)	Republic of China (1912-1949)	People's Republic of China (1949-)

Li Shizhen

Ming pharmacist Li Shizhen (1518-1593) was the author of the *Compendium of Materia Medica*. With 1,111 exquisite illustrations, the book incorporates 1,892 types of medicinal substances, including 374 new drugs he added himself, collecting 11,096 prescriptions, and offering a systematic summary of the achievements of Chinese medicine over thousands of years.

Li Zicheng

Li Zicheng (1606-1645), a peasant in northern Shaanxi, participated in a peasant uprising in 1620. In 1644, he led his troops to capture Beijing and overthrew the Ming Dynasty. Later, the Qing army broke through the Shanhai Pass and defeated Li Zicheng and his men; subsequently Li withdrew from Beijing, and died in Hubei.

Sun Yat-sen

Sun Yat-sen (1866-1925) was a pioneer of the Chinese democratic revolution. He set up the United Revolutionary League and put forward the "Three Principles of the People" — Nationalism, Democracy, and People's Livelihood. In 1911, Sun led the people to overthrow the Qing government, in what came to be known as the Revolution of 1911, and was elected provisional president of the Republic of China. In the following year he transformed his revolutionary organization into a political party, known as the Kuomintang (KMT, or Nationalist party). In 1924, Sun founded the Huangpu Military Academy, which trained and fostered many military and political talent, aimed at creating a revolutionary army to save an endangered China.

Some Key Events in Chinese History After the 17th Century

Recapture of Taiwan by Zheng Chenggong

In the early 17th century, the Dutch East India Company invaded Taiwan and made it a trade colony. In 1662, Chinese General Zheng Chenggong (1624-1662) recaptured Taiwan and the Penghu Islands (once called Pescadores by the Portuguese), establishing Chinese sovereignty there. In 1684, the Qing government set up Taiwan Prefecture and later set up the Taiwan Province, under the direct control of the Qing government.

First Opium War

Some Western countries forced China to open its doors by smuggling opium to China from the 19th century. Chinese official Lin Zexu burned nearly 1.2 million kg of opium in public at Humen, Guangdong, in 1839. On June 28, 1840, a British naval fleet blocked the mouth of the Pearl River, seized Xiamen, Shanghai and other port cities, and sailed up the Yangtze River to attack Nanjing.

Establishment of Dalai and Panchen Titles

In 1653, Qing Emperor Shunzhi conferred the title of Dalai Lama on the Fifth Dalai. In 1713, Qing Emperor Kangxi dispatched an envoy to confer the title of Panchen Erdeni on the Fifth Panchen. The Qing court also stipulated that the Dalai and Panchen lamas of later generations must be authorized by the Central Government. This system has been maintained to the present day.

Treaty of Nanjing

On August 29, 1842, when the British troops arrived at the city walls of Nanjing, the Qing government was forced to sign the unequal Treaty of Nanjing. According to the Treaty, China had to cede Hong Kong to Britain and open up five cities as treaty ports, as well as pay huge sums in reparations. The United States, France, Spain and Italy, in succession, obtained the same privileges by force. China was hence relegated to a semi-colony of the Western powers.

Second Opium War

From 1856 to 1860 the British and French allied fleet, supported by Russia and the United States, launched the Second Opium War on China and forced the Qing government to sign more unequal treaties with the four countries. Apart from enormous amounts in reparations, China lost large areas of territory. Yuanmingyuan (Garden of Perfection and Brightness), known as the "garden of gardens," was destroyed by the British and French allied forces.

Reform Movement

In 1898 Kang Youwei (1858-1927), along with others, staged a reform movement involving political, military, economic and cultural changes. They dreamed of establishing a constitutional monarchy in China through the support of the Qing government, to make the country strong and prosperous. The movement suffered sharp resistance from royal conservatives and was ended by a cruel massacre, after lasting a hundred days.

Westernization Movement

The Westernization Movement, from the 1860s to the mid-1890s, was initiated by the Qing government to learn from Western capitalist countries, in respect of military, political, economic, cultural, educational and diplomatic knowledge. Its activities included setting up military industry and related enterprises, equipping the army and navy with new-type weapons, and dispatching Chinese students to study in Europe and America. The Movement was intended to make China strong and prosperous, but ended in failure.

Revolution of 1911

The Revolution of 1911 was a democratic revolution led by Sun Yat-sen. In 1911, when the Qing government planned to give the authority for railway construction in China to foreign companies, forces from all quarters united to rise up and seize political power of southern provinces. On January 1, 1912, the provisional government of the Republic of China was founded in Nanjing. On February 12 that same year, the last Qing emperor was forced to abdicate, replacing the 2,000-year feudal monarchy with a republic.

Founding of the People's Republic of China

On October 1, 1949, in Beijing in a grand ceremony witnessed by crowds of Beijing people at Tiananmen Square, Mao Zedong, chairman of the Central People's Government, solemnly proclaimed the founding of the People's Republic of China. From then on, the CPC as the party in power began to administer New China, with the people as the masters of the country.

May 4th Movement

The May 4th Movement of 1919 is regarded as the ideological origin of many important events in modern Chinese history. Its direct cause was the unequal treaties imposed on China after the First World War. Motivated by strong patriotism, students initiated the movement, and it further developed into a national protest movement involving people from all walks of life. It also marked the introduction into China of various new ideologies, among which the spread of Marxism-Leninism is especially noteworthy.

The CPC and Mao Zedong

In 1921, 12 delegates, including Mao Zedong (1893-1976), representing communist groups in different places throughout the country, held the First National Congress in Shanghai to found the Communist Party of China (CPC). Today's CPC, with over 73 million members, is the mainstay of Chinese society. Mao Zedong, one of the founders of the CPC and the People's Republic of China, made extraordinary contributions to China's revolution and construction. He was a revolutionary, as well as a poet and calligrapher.

War of Resistance against Japanese Aggression

From 1937 to 1945 the Chinese people struggled hard against the aggression of Japanese imperialism and won the final victory, in what is known as the War of Resistance against Japanese Aggression. According to incomplete statistics, Chinese military and civilian casualties totaled over 35 million; and China's direct economic losses, from 1937 figures converted to current value, reached over US$ 100 billion, with indirect losses of over US$ 500 billion, as well as incalculable precious cultural heritage lost or destroyed through the war.

First Five-Year Plan

The First Five-Year Plan, implemented from 1953 to 1957, accomplished great achievements: the average annual increase rate in national income reached 8.9% and above; a number of basic industries necessary for national industrialization, until then non-existent domestically, were established, including producing airplanes, automobiles, heavy and precision machinery, power-generating equipment, metallurgical and mining equipment, high-grade alloy steels and non-ferrous metals. From that time on, the Chinese government set economic objectives and implemented a new five-year plan every five years. The 11th Five-Year Plan (2006-2010) is now under way.

The Return of Hong Kong and Macao to China: One Country, Two Systems

China resumed its sovereignty over Hong Kong and Macao on July 1 1997 and December 20 1999, respectively, establishing the Hong Kong Special Administrative Region (HKSAR) and Macao Special Administrative Region (MSAR). The Central Government has carried out the basic policies of "one country, two systems" and "a high degree of autonomy." "One country, two systems" refers to the fact that in China, a unified country, the socialist system is regarded as predominant, while the capitalist system and way of life in Hong Kong and Macao will be retained for 50 years.

"Cultural Revolution"

The "Cultural Revolution" (1966-1976) was a period of turmoil in China's modern history, bringing extensive damage to China's politics, economy, culture and people's lives. After the downfall of the "Gang of Four," the government under the leadership of Deng Xiaoping restored order out of the chaos and carried out policies of reform and opening-up, bringing China and the Chinese people on the road to modernization.

Reform and Opening up, and Deng Xiaoping

The Third Plenary Session of the 11th CPC Central Committee, held at the end of 1978, ushered in a new historic era for China. Chinese leader Deng Xiaoping (1904-1997) vigorously promoted the policy of reform and opening-up, and placed the national work focus on modernization. The road to modernization with Chinese characteristics was gradually established, through opening-up and reforms in the economic, political and cultural systems.

In 1992, Deng Xiaoping, the principal formulator of China's reform and opening-up, during his southern inspection made an important speech, becoming a key endorsement for economic reform and social progress in the following years.

Jiang Zemin and Hu Jintao became General Secretary of the CPC Central Committee in 1989 and in 2002, respectively. Both of them have inherited and developed the policy of reform and opening-up initiated by Deng Xiaoping, so that China has attained rapid economic growth and remarkable improvement of people's lives, attracting world attention.

Administrative Divisions
and Cities

Administrative Divisions

The whole country is divided into provinces, autonomous regions and municipalities directly under the Central Government.

A province or an autonomous region is further subdivided into cities (autonomous prefectures) and counties (autonomous counties).

Municipalities directly under the Central Government and large cities are subdivided into districts and counties.

Autonomous prefectures are subdivided into counties, autonomous counties and cities.

Counties and autonomous counties are subdivided into townships, ethnic townships and towns.

Autonomous regions, autonomous prefectures and autonomous counties are all autonomous ethnic minority areas.

The state will establish special administrative regions when necessary. The system implemented in special administrative regions will be stipulated by law, as set by the NPC according to actual conditions.

At present, there are 23 provinces, 5 autonomous regions, 4 municipalities directly under the Central Government, and 2 special administrative regions.

Administrative Map of China

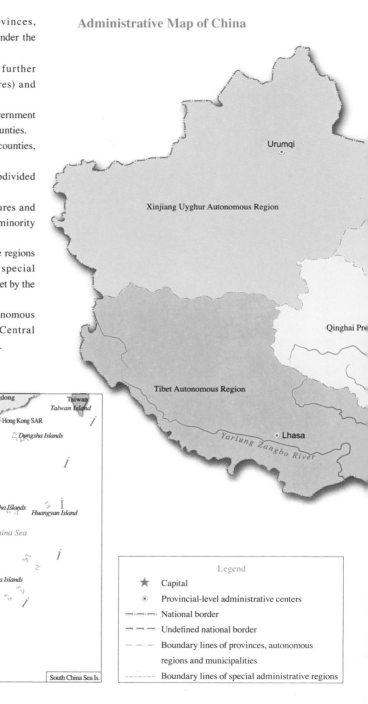

Legend	
★	Capital
⊙	Provincial-level administrative centers
·—··—··—	National border
— — —	Undefined national border
—··—··—	Boundary lines of provinces, autonomous regions and municipalities
—·····—	Boundary lines of special administrative regions

Proportion of Provinces, Autonomous Regions
and Municipalities in National Territory Areas

Province
Municipality
Autonomous region
Special administrative region

Heilongjiang Province

Heilong River

⊙Harbin

⊙Changchun
Jilin Province

Shenyang⊙
Liaoning Province

Inner Mongolia Autonomous Region

Province

Hohhot
⊙

Hebei Province

Beijing
Beijing
Municipality

★

Tianjin⊙
Tianjin
Municipality

Bohai Sea

⊙Yinchuan

Ningxia Hui
Autonomous
Region

Taiyuan
⊙

Shijiazhuang
⊙

Xining⊙

Lanzhou
⊙

Shanxi Province

River

Yellow River

⊙Jinan
Shandong Province

Yellow Sea

Shaanxi Province
⊙

Zhengzhou
⊙

Xi'an⊙

Henan Province

Jiangsu Province

Anhui Province

Nanjing
⊙

Shanghai
Municipality
Shanghai

Hefei
⊙

Sichuan Province

Yangtze River

Hubei Province

Yangtze River

Chengdu⊙

Wuhan
⊙

Hangzhou⊙

East China Sea

Chongqing⊙
Chongqing
Municipality

Zhejiang Province

Changsha
⊙

Nanchang
⊙

Guizhou Province

Hunan Province

Jiangxi Province

Chiwei Island

⊙Guiyang

Fuzhou
⊙
Fujian Province

Taibei⊙

Diaoyu Island

Kunming⊙

nan Province

Guangxi Zhuang
Autonomous Region

Guangdong Province

Guangzhou

Taiwan Province
Taiwan Island

Taiwan Strait

Penghu Islands

⊙Nanning

Pearl River

Hong Kong
Macao⊙ ⊙Hong Kong SAR
Macao SAR

Dongsha Islands

⊙Haikou
Hainan Province
Hainan Island

South China Sea

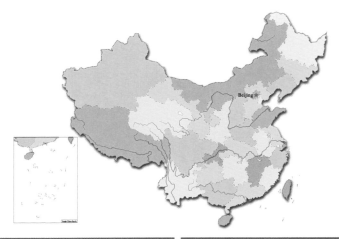

Beijing

Area	16,800 sq km
Population	16.33 million
Population density	972 persons/sq km
Average life expectancy	78.01
Total output value	906.62 billion yuan
Main agriculture	vegetable, fruit
Cultivated area	343,900 hectares
Main industries	telecommunications and electronics, IT
Railways	1,121.5 km
Highways	20,503 km
Main mineral deposits	coal, iron, limestone
Export volume	48.92 billion US$
College students (per m. persons)	68,970
Inbound visitors	3.826 million

Tianjin

Area	11,300 sq km
Population	11.15 million
Population density	87.76 persons/sq.km
Average life expectancy	76.63
Total output value	501.828 billion yuan
Main agriculture	wheat, corn, paddy rice
Cultivated area	485,600 hectares
Main industry	petrol products, light textiles
Railways	744.7 km
Highways	11,316 km
Main mineral deposits	chambersite, manganese, gold
Export volume	38.15 billion US$
College students (per m. persons)	46,000
Inbound visitors	952,000

Shanghai

Area	6,340.5 sq km
Population	18.58 million
Population density	2930.37 persons/sq.km
Average life expectancy	80.04
Total output value	1200.116 billion yuan
Main agriculture	paddy rice, rapeseed, flower
Cultivated area	315,100 hectares
Main industry	various industries
Railways	310.3 km
Highways	10,392 km
Main mineral deposits	subterranean oil and gas resources
Export volume	143.89 billion US$
College students (per m. persons)	42,060
Inbound visitors	4.426 million

Chongqing

Area	82,300 sq km
Population	28.16 million
Population density	342.16 persons/sq.km
Average life expectancy	73.89
Total output value	411.182 billion yuan
Main agriculture	paddy rice, wheat, rapeseed, tea
Cultivated area	1,384,000 hectares
Main industry	automobile, medicine, food
Railways	1,261.9 km
Highways	100,299 km
Main mineral deposits	strontium, manganese, vanadium
Export volume	4.508 billion US$
College students (per m. persons)	19,060
Inbound visitors	622,000

Inner Mongolia (Capital city: Hohhot)

Area	1,197,500 sq km
Population	24.05 million
Population density	20.08 persons/sq.km
Average life expectancy	71.79
Total output value	601.881 billion yuan
Main agriculture	wheat, beet, animal husbandry
Cultivated area	8,201,000 hectares
Main industry	iron and steel, coal mining, metallurgy
Railways	6,382.6 km
Highways	128,762 km
Main mineral deposits	thulium, coal, silver
Export volume	2.948 billion US$
College students (per m. persons)	14,130
Inbound visitors	1.474 million

Guangxi (Capital city: Nanning)

Area	237,700 sq km
Population	47.68 million
Population density	200.59 persons/sq.km
Average life expectancy	73.75
Total output value	588.588 billion yuan
Main agriculture	sugarcane, flue-cured tobacco, cassava
Cultivated area	4,407,900 hectares
Main industry	sugar refining
Railways	2,735.2 km
Highways	90,318 km
Main mineral deposits	indium, manganese, tin
Export volume	5.113 billion US$
College students (per m. persons)	12,280
Inbound visitors	1.245 million

Tibet (Capital city: Lhasa)

Area	1,274,900 sq km
Population	2.85 million
Population density	2.24 persons/sq.km
Average life expectancy	66.15
Total output value	34.219 billion yuan
Main agriculture	paddy rice, highland barley
Cultivated area	362,600 hectares
Main industry	cement, Tibetan medicine
Railways	550 km
Highways	44,813 km
Main mineral deposits	copper, lithium
Export volume	326 million US$
College students (per m. persons)	10,140
Inbound visitors	339,000

Ningxia (Capital city: Yinchuan)

Area	62,800 sq km
Population	6.1025 million
Population density	97.17 persons/sq.km
Average life expectancy	71.84
Total output value	83.416 billion yuan
Main agriculture	paddy rice, wheat
Cultivated area	1,268,800 hectares
Main industry	coal, electricity
Railways	789 km
Highways	19,903 km
Main mineral deposits	coal, silex, gypsum
Export volume	1.089 million US$
College students (per m. persons)	15,110
Inbound visitors	7,800

Xinjiang (Capital city: Urumqi)

Area	1,655,800 sq km
Population	20.9519 million
Population density	12.65 persons/sq.km
Average life expectancy	69.14
Total output value	349.442 billion yuan
Main agriculture	wheat, cotton, benne, fruit
Cultivated area	3,985,700 hectares
Main industries	textile, petrochemicals
Railways	2,760.8 km
Highways	143,736 km
Main mineral deposits	coal, petroleum, natural gas
Export volume	11.503 billion US$
College students (per m. persons)	14,160
Inbound visitors	313,100

Hebei (Capital city: Shijiazhuang)

Area	187,700 sq km
Population	69.432 million
Population density	369.90 persons/sq.km
Average life expectancy	74.57
Total output value	1,386.35 billion yuan
Main agriculture	wheat, corn, bean, fruit
Cultivated area	6,883,300 hectares
Main industries	iron and steel, equipment, petrochemicals
Railways	4,818.2 km
Highways	143,778 km
Main mineral deposits	34 minerals ranking first 5 in the country
Export volume	17.02 billion US$
College students (per m. persons)	16,300
Inbound visitors	654,000

Shanxi (Capital city: Taiyuan)

Area	156,000 sq km
Population	33.9258 million
Population density	217.47 persons/sq.km
Average life expectancy	73.57
Total output value	569.62 billion yuan
Main agriculture	wheat, corn, cotton
Cultivated area	4,588,600 hectares
Main industry	coal, metallurgy
Railways	3,110.4 km
Highways	112,930 km
Main mineral deposits	coal, iron, bauxite
Export volume	6.53296 billion US$
College students (per m. persons)	17,900
Inbound visitors	330,200

Liaoning (Capital city: Shenyang)

Area	145,900 sq km
Population	42.98 million
Population density	294.58 persons/sq.km
Average life expectancy	75.36
Total output value	1102.17 billion yuan
Main agriculture	paddy rice, wheat, corn, bean
Cultivated area	8,201,000 hectares
Main industry	aviation, automobile, iron and steel, equipment
Railways	4,196.3 km
Highways	97,786 km
Main mineral deposits	iron, manganese, petroleum, natural gas
Export volume	35.325 billion US$
College students (per m. persons)	23,790
Inbound visitors	1,372,500

Jilin (Capital city: Changchun)

Area	187,400 sq km
Population	27.2982 million
Population density	145.67 persons/sq.km
Average life expectancy	75.04
Total output value	522.608 billion yuan
Main agriculture	rice, soybean, corn, potato
Cultivated area	5,578,400 hectares
Main industry	automobile, equipment
Railways	3,555.4 km
Highways	84,444 km
Main mineral deposits	oil shale, diatomaceous earth
Export volume	3.858 billion US$
College students (per m. persons)	23,590
Inbound visitors	354,300

Heilongjiang (Capital city: Harbin)

Area	460,000 sq km
Population	38.23 million
Population density	83.13 persons/sq.km
Average life expectancy	74.66
Total output value	707.72 billion yuan
Main agriculture	wheat, soybean, beet
Cultivated area	11,773,000 hectares
Main industry	equipment, machine building industry, petrochemicals
Railways	5,654.3 km
Highways	139,335 km
Main mineral deposits	coal, petroleum, gold
Export volume	12.27 billion US$
College students (per m. persons)	20,900
Inbound visitors	994,800

Jiangsu (Capital city: Nanjing)

Area	102,600 sq km
Population	76.245 million
Population density	743 persons/sq.km
Average life expectancy	76.23
Total output value	2,556.01 billion yuan
Main agriculture	rapeseed, paddy rice, silkworm, fishery
Cultivated area	5,061,700 hectares
Main industry	machinery, electronics, textile, silk
Railways	1,616.1 km
Highways	126,972 km
Main mineral deposits	calcite, marl
Export volume	203.73 billion US$
College students (per m. persons)	23,010
Inbound visitors	3,148,800

Zhejiang (Capital city: Hangzhou)

Area	101,800 sq km
Population	50.6 million
Population density	497.05 persons/sq.km
Average life expectancy	77.21
Total output value	1,863.84 billion yuan
Main agriculture	rice, tea, silkworm, aquatic products
Cultivated area	2,125,300 hectares
Main industry	pharmaceuticals, chemical textile, silk
Railways	1,278.5 km
Highways	95,310 km
Main mineral deposits	stone coal, alum-stone
Export volume	128.3 billion US$
College students (per m. persons)	21,150
Inbound visitors	2,813,700

Anhui (Capital city: Hefei)

Area	139,600 sq km
Population	66.757 million
Population density	428.2 persons/sq.km
Average life expectancy	73.59
Total output value	734.57 billion yuan
Main agriculture	paddy rice, wheat, cotton, tea
Cultivated area	5,971,700 hectares
Main industry	coal, metallurgy, textile, foodstuff
Railways	2,387 km
Highways	147,611 km
Main mineral deposits	coal, iron, copper, sulfur
Export volume	8.82 billion US$
College students (per m. persons)	13,510
Inbound visitors	525,900

Fujian (Capital city: Fuzhou)

Area	121,400 sq km
Population	35.81 million
Population density	294.98 persons/sq.km
Average life expectancy	72.55
Total output value	916.014 billion yuan
Main agriculture	fruit, flower
Cultivated area	1,434,700 hectares
Main industry	shipping, hydropower
Railways	1,612.8 km
Highways	86,560 km
Main mineral deposits	quartz sand
Export volume	49.943 billion US$
College students (per m. persons)	16,560
Inbound visitors	789,700

Jiangxi (Capital city: Nanchang)

Area	166,900 sq km
Population	43.6841 million
Population density	261.74 persons/sq.km
Average life expectancy	68.95
Total output value	546.93 billion yuan
Main agriculture	paddy rice, oilseed, freshwater fish
Cultivated area	2,993,400 hectares
Main industry	machinery, electronics
Railways	2,423.7 km
Highways	128,236 km
Main mineral deposits	copper, tungsten, gold, silver
Export volume	5.46 billion US$
College students (per m. persons)	21,050
Inbound visitors	184,100

Shandong (Capital city: Jinan)

Area	156,700 sq km
Population	93.67 million
Population density	597.77 persons/sq.km
Average life expectancy	73.92
Total output value	2,588.77 billion yuan
Main agriculture	wheat, corn, peanut, fruit
Cultivated area	7,689,300 hectares
Main industry	energy, foodstuff
Railways	3,329.2 km
Highways	204,910 km
Main mineral deposits	gold, coal, crude oil
Export volume	75.24 billion US$
College students (per m. persons)	18,110
Inbound visitors	1,560,400

Henan (Capital city: Zhengzhou)

Area	167,000 sq km
Population	98.69 million
Population density	590.96 persons/sq.km
Average life expectancy	71.45
Total output value	1,505.807 billion yuan
Main agriculture	wheat, corn, cotton
Cultivated area	8,110,300 hectares
Main industry	foodstuff, machinery
Railways	4,038.7 km
Highways	236,351 km
Main mineral deposits	molybdenum, cyanite
Export volume	8.391 billion US$
College students (per m. persons)	11,310
Inbound visitors	453,900

Hubei (Capital city: Wuhan)

Area	185,900 sq km
Population	60.7 million
Population density	326.52 persons/sq.km
Average life expectancy	71.08
Total output value	915.001 billion yuan
Main agriculture	paddy rice, wheat, cotton, oilseed
Cultivated area	4,949,500 hectares
Main industry	iron and steel, machinery
Railways	2,527.0 km
Highways	181,791 km
Main mineral deposits	phosphorus, rutile, wollastonite
Export volume	8.174 billion US$
College students (per m. persons)	25,420
Inbound visitors	857,000

Hunan (Capital city: Changsha)

Area	211,800 sq km
Population	68.057 million
Population density	321.33 persons/sq.km
Average life expectancy	70.66
Total output value	914.5 billion yuan
Main agriculture	paddy rice, ramie, flue-cured tobacco
Cultivated area	3,953,000 hectares
Main industries	metallurgy, machinery
Railways	2,905.6 km
Highways	171,848 km
Main mineral deposits	tungsten, bismuth
Export volume	6.523 billion US$
College students (per m. persons)	17,190
Inbound visitors	731,100

Guangdong (Capital city: Guangzhou)

Area	178,000 sq km
Population	94.49 million
Population density	530.84 persons/sq.km
Average life expectancy	73.27
Total output value	3,067.371 billion yuan
Main agriculture	paddy rice, sugarcane, peanut, fruit
Cultivated area	3,272,200 hectares
Main industry	electronics, home appliance
Railways	2,167.9 km
Highways	178,387 km
Main mineral deposits	kaolin, peat
Export volume	369.246 billion US$
College students (per m. persons)	15,910
Inbound visitors	5,346,500

Hainan (Capital city: Haikou)

Area	35,000 sq km
Population	8.4503 million
Population density	241.44 persons/sq.km
Average life expectancy	72.92
Total output value	122.96 billion yuan
Main agriculture	sugarcane, paddy rice, rubber
Cultivated area	762,100 hectares
Main industry	light industry, chemicals
Railways	224.1 km
Highways	17,577 km
Main mineral deposits	glass sand
Export volume	1.838 billion US$
College students (per m. persons)	13,740
Inbound visitors	465,700

Sichuan (Capital city: Chengdu)

Area	485,000 sq km
Population	81.27 million
Population density	167.57 persons/sq.km
Average life expectancy	71.20
Total output value	1,050.53 billion yuan
Main agriculture	paddy rice, cotton, oilseed, natural silk
Cultivated area	9,169,100 hectares
Main industry	metallurgy, chemical industry, textile, foodstuff
Railways	2,986.0 km
Highways	182,000 km
Main mineral deposits	vanadium, titanium, calcium
Export volume	8.61 billion US$
College students (per m. persons)	14,140
Inbound visitors	857,600

Guizhou (Capital city: Guiyang)

Area	176,100 sq km
Population	39.7548 million
Population density	225.75 persons/sq.km
Average life expectancy	65.63
Total output value	271.028 billion yuan
Main agriculture	paddy rice, flue-cured tobacco, tung trees
Cultivated area	4,903,500 hectares
Main industry	water conservancy, mining
Railways	2,013.6 km
Highways	113,278 km
Main mineral deposits	mercury, barite
Export volume	1.465 billion US$
College students (per m. persons)	9,100
Inbound visitors	107,000

Yunnan (Capital city: Kunming)

Area	394,000 sq km
Population	45.14 million
Population density	114.57 persons/sq.km
Average life expectancy	65.49
Total output value	472.177 billion yuan
Main agriculture	paddy rice, corm, flower, flue-cured tobacco
Cultivated area	6,421,600 hectares
Main industry	light industry, foodstuff, electricity
Railways	2,309.8 km
Highways	198,496 km
Main mineral deposits	copper, tin
Export volume	4.736 billion US$
College students (per m. persons)	10,420
Inbound visitors	1,111,700

Shaanxi (Capital city: Xi'an)

Area	205,600 sq km
Population	37.48 million
Population density	182.30 persons/sq.km
Average life expectancy	70.07
Total output value	536.985 billion yuan
Main agriculture	paddy rice, wheat, legumes
Cultivated area	5,140,500 hectares
Main industry	oil, natural gas, coal
Railways	3,184.9 km
Highways	113,303 km
Main mineral deposits	coal, petroleum, natural gas
Export volume	4.672 billion US$
College students (per m. persons)	25,490
Inbound visitors	831,600

Gansu (Capital city: Lanzhou)

Area	454,400 sq km
Population	26.1716 million
Population density	57.60 persons/sq.km
Average life expectancy	64.47
Total output value	269.92 billion yuan
Main agriculture	wheat, corn, benne
Cultivated area	5,024,700 hectares
Main industry	nonferrous metal, petrochemical industry
Railways	2,435.4 km
Highways	95,642 km
Main mineral deposits	coal, petroleum, natural gas
Export volume	1.659 billion US$
College students (per m. persons)	14,270
Inbound visitors	184,600

Qinghai (Capital city: Xining)

Area	721,200 sq km
Population	5.516 million
Population density	7.65 persons/sq.km
Average life expectancy	66.03
Total output value	76.096 billion yuan
Main agriculture	wheat, highland barley, rapeseed
Cultivated area	688,000 hectares
Main industry	electricity, crude oil, crude salt
Railways	1,652.4 km
Highways	47,726 km
Main mineral deposits	kalium, natrium, magnesium, lithium
Export volume	386 million US$
College students (per m. persons)	9,350
Inbound visitors	27,700

Taiwan

Area	36,006 sq km
Population	22.95 million
Population density	632.20 persons/sq.km
Average life expectancy	male: 74.05 female: 80.21
Total output value	374.5 billion US$
Main agriculture	rice, sugarcane, tea, fruit
Cultivated area	67,800 hectares
Main industry	textile, electronics, sugar refining
Railways	2,502 km
Highways	37,299 km
Main mineral deposits	gold, copper, petroleum, natural gas
Export volume	224 billion US$
College students (per m. persons)	234,823
Inbound visitors	3.52 million

Hong Kong (Special Administrative Region)

Area	1,104.00 sq km
Population	6.9217 million
Population density	6,211.05 persons/sq.km
Average life expectancy	male: 79.5 female: 85.6
Total output value	289.7 billion US$
Main agriculture	vegetable, flower, fruit
Cultivated area	5,900 hectares
Main industry	electronics, textiles, garment
Railways	200 km
Highways	2,009 km
Main mineral deposits	iron, aluminum, zinc, tungsten
Export volume	316.645 billion US$
College students (per m. persons)	188,300
Inbound visitors	28 million

Macao (Special Administrative Region)

Area	28.6 sq km
Population	531,400 million
Population density	17,447.55 persons/sq.km
Average life expectancy	male: 77.6 female: 82.3
Total output value	14.29 billion US$
Main agriculture	vegetable, flower
Cultivated area	
Main industry	toy, garment
Railways	
Highways	368 km
Main mineral deposits	granite
Export volume	291.10 billion US$
College students (per m. persons)	25,907
Inbound visitors	27 million

Hong Kong Special Administrative Region

The Hong Kong Special Administrative Region (HKSAR) is located on the east side of the estuary of the Pearl River. The city area covers 1,104 sq km. In 2007, the population in Hong Kong reached 6,921,700.

Hong Kong was occupied by Britain after the Opium War of 1840. In accordance with the "Sino-British Joint Declaration on the Question of Hong Kong," signed in 1984, China resumed its exercise of sovereignty over Hong Kong on July 1, 1997, when the Hong Kong Special Administrative Region of the People's Republic of China was formally established. The Chinese government has carried out the basic policies of "one country, two systems," "administration of Hong Kong by the Hong Kong people," and "a high degree of autonomy" in Hong Kong. "One country, two systems" refers to the fact that in China, a unified country, the mainland practices the socialist system, while Hong Kong retains its original capitalist system and way of life unchanged for 50 years; "administration of Hong Kong by the Hong Kong people" means that the HKSAR is administered by the Hong Kong people on their own, enjoying "a high degree of autonomy." The HKSAR shall fully enjoy autonomous administrative, legislative, independent judicial and final adjudication powers. The present Chief Executive of HKSAR is Donald Tsang Yam-kuen.

The design on HKSAR's regional flag is a blossoming bauhinia.

Hong Kong's economy is remarkable for its free trade, low tax rates and minimum interference by the government. Its rank in the global trade and economic system is 13th, and its main trading partner is China's mainland. The Global Financial Centers Index (GFCI) published by the city of London indicates that Hong Kong's rank in GFCI is third in the world, only behind London and New York.

In 2007, the total GDP of Hong Kong was US$ 289.7 billion. The per-capita GDP is US$ 41,614.

The Chinese and British governments holding the ceremony for the transfer of Hong Kong sovereignty, in the Hong Kong Convention and Exhibition Center, from midnight June 30 to the early hours of July 1, 1997

Macao Special Administrative Region

The Macao Special Administrative Region (MSAR) is located on the west side of the estuary of the Pearl River with a total area of 28.6 sq km and population of 531,400.

Macao was occupied by Portugal after the Opium War of 1840. In accordance with the "Sino-Portugal Joint Declaration on the Question of Macao," signed in 1987, China resumed its sovereignty over Macao on December 20, 1999, when the Macao Special Administrative Region was formally established. The Chinese government has carried out the basic policies of "one country, two systems," "administration of Macao by the Macao people," and "a high degree of autonomy" in Macao. "One country, two systems" refers to the fact that in China, a unified country, the mainland practices the socialist system, while Macao retains its original capitalist system and way of life unchanged for 50 years; "administration of Macao by the Macao people" means that the MSAR is administered by the Macao people on their own, enjoying "a high degree of autonomy." The MSAR fully enjoys the power of decision over matters within their autonomous jurisdiction, including administrative, legislative, independent judicial and final adjudication powers. The present Chief Executive of MSAR is Ho Hau-Wah. The design on MSAR's regional flag is a lotus flower in bloom.

As one of two international free trade ports in China, Macao enjoys full FIO rights in cargo, capital, foreign currencies and personnel. The tourism industry is its key economic pillar. The number of visitors to Macao is over 20 million every year. In 2007, the number of visitors to Macao reached 27 million person-times, with a 22.8% annual increase.

The tourist and casino industry is indispensable to Macao, hence the name "Monte Carlo of the East." In 2007, gross revenue from this industry surpassed 83.847 billion Macao patacas (US$ 10.48 billion), and payment of direct taxes reached 29.34 billion Macao patacas (US$ 3.668 billion).

The Chinese and Portuguese governments holding the ceremony for the transfer of Macao sovereignty, in the Macao Cultural Center, from midnight December 19 to the early hours of December 20, 1999

Taiwan

Taiwan is an inseparable part of China's territory. Located by the southeast coastal continental shelf of China's mainland, it is the largest island in China, covering an area of 36,006 sq km, with a population of 22.95 million (as of end of 2007).

In 1993, China's mainland and Taiwan held Wang Daohan-Koo Chen-fu Talks (Wang-Koo talks) in Singapore.

Records of Chinese people developing Taiwan in earlier periods have been found in many historical books and documents. Beginning from the mid-12th century, the governments of different Chinese dynasties had set up administrative bodies to exercise jurisdiction over Taiwan. Japan started the First Sino-Japanese War in 1894, after which the Qing government was forced to sign the humiliating Treaty of Maguan (Simonoseki) with Japan in April 1895, which ceded Taiwan and Penghu Islands to Japan. In July 1937, Japan launched a new Sino-Japanese War, marking the beginning of Chinese people's national resistance against Japanese aggression. On 15 August 1945, Japan was defeated and forced into an unconditional surrender. The Chinese people thus won the War of Resistance against Japanese Aggression, recovering Taiwan and Penghu Islands. In 1949, the Kuomintang authorities lost the civil war, and retreated to Taiwan, in confrontation with China's mainland. In 1950, the Korean War broke out, and the United States dispatched its Seventh Fleet to the Taiwan Straits, openly interfering in China's internal affairs and obstructing the liberation of Taiwan. In 1971, the 26th session of the UN General Assembly restored the legitimate rights of the People's Republic of China in the United Nations. On 1 January 1979, the United States established official diplomatic relations with China, formally recognizing the government of the PRC as the sole legitimate government of China, and that there is but one China, with Taiwan as part of China. Subsequently, however, the US Congress passed the Taiwan Relations Act, resulting in fierce opposition from the Chinese government. But the US has gradually realized the importance of Sino-US relations. US leaders have stated many times that they adhere to the "one-China" policy, observe the Three Sino-US Joint Communiqués and do not support "Taiwan independence."

Since the publication on 1 January 1979, by the NPC Standing Committee, of the "Appeal to Compatriots in Taiwan," the Central Government has resolutely implemented the basic policy of "peaceful reunification, and one country, two systems," and actively promoted people-to-people contacts and bilateral exchanges in the fields of economy, culture, etc. In 1992, the mainland's Association for Relations Across the Taiwan Straits and Taiwan's Straits Exchange Foundation reached a verbal agreement that "both sides of the Taiwan Straits adhere to the one-China principle." The "Wang (Daohan)–Koo (Chen-fu) Talk" held in 1993 signaled a historically important step forward in the development of cross-Straits relations.

From the mid-1990s, Taiwan leader Lee Teng-hui embarked on a road to split the country. In 1999, he openly claimed that the relationship between the mainland and Taiwan was a "special country-to-country relation," doing great damage to relations across the Straits. Since assuming office in 2000, Chen Shui-bian of the Democratic Progressive Party (DPP), who advocates "Taiwan independence," accelerated secessionist activities. He asserted a "one country on each side" claim and a "Taiwan independence timetable," clamored for "de jure independence" through "constitutional reform," and a "referendum on joining the UN under the name of Taiwan." The Chinese government and people fought resolutely and powerfully against the secessionist activities of "Taiwan independence" forces, thwarting their conspiracy of "de jure independence". The DPP lost the Taiwan legislative election held in January 12, 2008 as well as the election of the Taiwan area leader held in March 22, and the "referendum on joining the UN" pushed hard by the DPP also met its Waterloo, demonstrating the failure of "Taiwan independence."

Taipei 101

The CPC and the government of the PRC have made unremitting efforts to resolve the issue of Taiwan and realize the reunification of the country, putting forward the basic policy of "peaceful reunification, and one country, two systems," based on the fundamental interests of China and the Chinese nation. On January 30, 1995, Jiang Zemin, then General Secretary of the CPC Central Committee and President of the PRC, delivered an important speech, entitled "Continue to Fight for Fulfillment of the Great Cause of Reunification of the Motherland," putting forward eight proposals to develop relations between the two sides and promote the reunification of the country. On March 4, 2005, Hu Jintao, General Secretary of the CPC Central Committee and President of the PRC, put forward four points on cross-Straits relations under the new situation, including never giving up on efforts to seek peaceful reunification and never compromising in opposing "Taiwan independence" secessionist activities. In March 2005, the Third Session of the 10th NPC ratified the Anti-Secession Law with an overwhelming vote, legalizing the Central Authorities' policy guidelines on Taiwan. The law also demonstrates that the entire Chinese people will safeguard China's sovereignty and territorial integrity, and never allow the "Taiwan independence" forces to separate Taiwan from China under any name or by any means. In April 2005, President Hu Jintao met visiting Lien Chan, Chairman of the Chinese Kuomintang, and then in May James Soong, Chairman of the People-First Party, putting forward important propositions on the building of a peaceful and steadily developing relationship between the two sides. In April 2006, President Hu Jintao again met Lien Chan, pointing out that "peace and development should be the theme of cross-Straits relations, and the common goal of the people both in the mainland and Taiwan." When speaking on the development of cross-Straits relations on March 4, 2008, President Hu Jintao stressed: "We will sincerely work for the well-being of our compatriots and peace of the area on both sides of the Straits. We are ready to have exchange, dialogue, consultation and negotiation with any political parties in Taiwan, as long as they recognize that both sides of the Taiwan Straits belong to one and the same China. Negotiations will be conducted on an equal footing with completely open topics, and there is nothing we cannot talk about." On April 29, President Hu Jintao said when meeting Lien Chan that the two sides of the Straits should work together to build mutual trust, put aside disputes, seek common ground while shelving differences, and create a win-win situation.

On April 19, 2007, Lien Chan, honorary chairman of Chinese Kuomintang, and his wife attended an ancestor worshipping ceremony in Xinzheng City, Henan Province, to pay respects to the Yellow Emperor.

On the afternoon of May 28, 2008, Hu Jintao held talks with Chinese Kuomintang Chairman Wu Poh-hsiung in Beijing. He emphasized that, owing to the joint efforts of Kuomintang and the CPC as well as compatriots across the Taiwan Straits, positive changes have emerged in the Taiwan situation, with the development of cross-Straits relations facing a hard-earned historical opportunity. This favorable situation has not been easily achieved and merits our doubled efforts to value fully. We wish Kuomintang and the CPC and the two sides across the Straits to be able to together work diligently to build mutual trust, put aside disputes, seek common grounds while shelving differences, and create a win-win situation; to continue to follow and fulfill "the common wish for peaceful development of the two sides of the Straits," to make effective efforts to promote cross-Straits relations with even more substantial achievements, and to strengthen Taiwan compatriots' confidence in the peaceful development of cross-Straits relations.

Commercial Exchange

For over 20 years, from 1987 until now, through mutual efforts by compatriots of both sides across the Taiwan Straits, people-to-people contacts and exchanges and cooperation in the fields of economy, trade, culture, etc., have been deepening day by day. By the end of 2007, the total trade volume across the Straits reached US$ 728.17 billion, in which Taiwan's favorable balance of trade reached US$ 476.32 billion; the total number of companies with Taiwan investment in the mainland came to 75,000, while the amount of actual utilization of Taiwanese investment was US$ 45.7 billion; and the visits of Taiwan residents to the mainland surpassed 47.03 million, and of mainland residents to Taiwan reached over 1.63 million.

Shanghai Pudong New Area

Urbanization Process

China had 656 cities by the end of 2007, including four municipalities directly under the Central Government, 283 prefecture-level cities and 368 county-level ones. Of the four municipalities and the prefecture-level cities, 13 had populations of more than four million in the urban area; 24 had between two and four million; 80 had between one and two million; 106 had between 500,000 and one million; 59 had between 200,000 and 500,000; and five had less than 200,000.

According to experts' predictions, there will be 10 major city clusters in China in the 21st century. Located in coastal areas, hinterland and border areas of the inland, they will become the best regions for potential development. Among them, the Beijing-Tianjin-Hebei-Province (Jing-Jin-Ji) Region, Yangtze River Delta Region and Pearl River Delta Region have already become China's leading economic regions by the end of 20th century, and will continue leading in economic development in the next 20 years. It is predicted that China's urbanization level will hit 65% by the mid-21st century.

In the face of highly accelerated urbanization, the Central Government has allocated

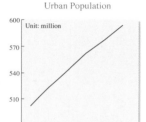

Urban Population

Unit: million

Suzhou Industrial Park, Jiangsu Province

and coordinated population, land, environment, and economic and social development by making strategic regional planning, while working hard to keep the urbanization process orderly. In the course of city planning, China has implemented the principle of "strict control over the size of large cities, rational development of medium-sized cities, and active development of small cities." Medium-sized cities with populations of between 200,000 and 500,000 and small cities with populations fewer than 200,000 have grown rapidly since the 1980s, while large cities with populations of over one million have developed satellite cities and towns in a planned and positive way.

Old City God Temple of Shanghai

Downtown of Shenzhen, Guangdong Province

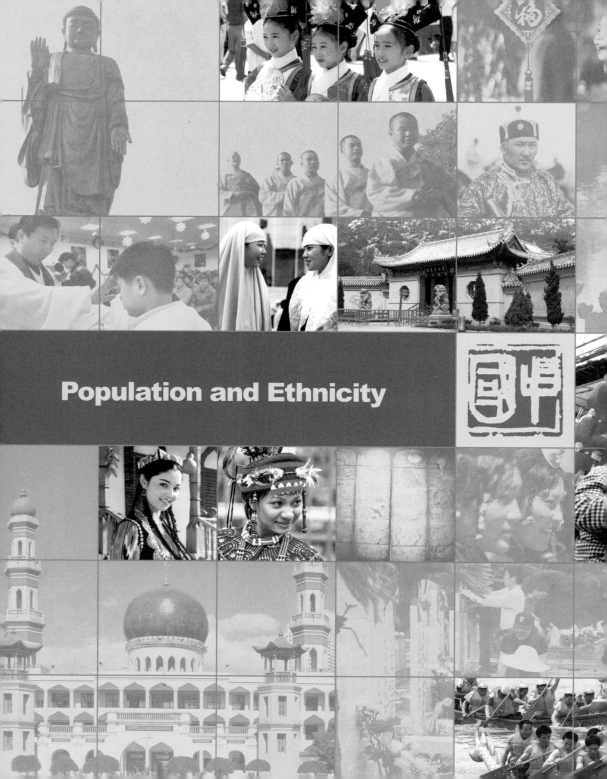

Population and Ethnicity

Population

China is the most populous country in the world, with 1.32129 billion people by the end of 2007, about one fifth of the world's total population. This figure does not include the Chinese living in the Hong Kong and Macao special administrative regions, and Taiwan Province.

Moreover, population density is high, with 138 people per sq km. This population, however, is unevenly distributed. The eastern coastal areas are densely populated, with more than 400 people per sq km; in the central areas this figure is over 200; while in the sparsely populated plateaus in the west there are less than 10 people per sq km.

The following table gives an overall view of the composition of the population:

Average life expectancy: 73.0
Birth rate: 12.10‰
Mortality: 6.93‰
Infant mortality: 15.3‰

(Not including Hong Kong, Macao and Taiwan Province)

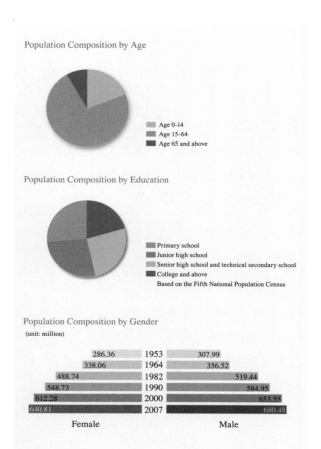

Population Composition by Age

- Age 0-14
- Age 15-64
- Age 65 and above

Population Composition by Education

- Primary school
- Junior high school
- Senior high school and technical secondary school
- College and above

Based on the Fifth National Population Census

Population Composition by Gender
(unit: million)

Female	Year	Male
286.36	1953	307.99
338.06	1964	356.52
488.74	1982	519.44
548.73	1990	584.95
612.28	2000	653.55
640.81	2007	680.48

Population Density
(persons/sq km)

- Above 600
- 400-600
- 100-400
- 50-100
- 1-50
- Below 1

Total Urban Population

2006
2000
1991

12 m.
9 m.
6 m.
3 m.

South China Sea Is.

Sketch Map Showing Distribution of Population Density

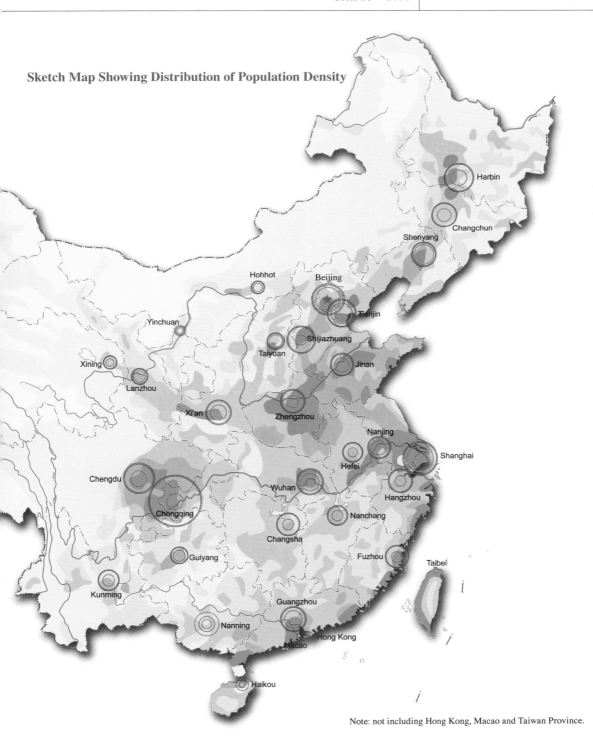

Note: not including Hong Kong, Macao and Taiwan Province.

Family Planning

Family planning has been one of China's basic state policies, combining government guidance with voluntary compliance of citizens. The central and local governments have instituted policies and regulations for controlling population growth, improving population quality and structure, as well as macro plans on population development. Governments should also provide consultation, guidance and technical services concerning reproductive care, contraception, healthy birth and positive childrearing. Couples of child-bearing age, guided by relevant state policies and regulations, can make arrangements for pregnancy and birth in an appropriate and responsible manner and choose appropriate contraceptive methods, taking their age, health, employment and financial situations into consideration.

The basic requirements of family planning: late marriage and late childbearing, having fewer but healthier babies, especially one child per couple. But a flexible practice is adopted for rural people and ethnic minorities. In rural areas, couples may have a second baby in exceptional cases, but must wait several years after the birth of the first child. In areas inhabited by minority peoples, each community may work out its own regulations in accordance with its wishes, population, natural resources, economy, culture and customs. In general couples may have a second baby, or a third in some places. As for ethnic minorities with extremely small populations, couples may have as many children as they wish.

An Aging Society

According to experts' analysis, China will become an aging society in the 21st century. The total population aged over 60 will reach nearly 300 million by 2025. Facing severe problems caused by an aging society, governments at all levels in China are adopting a positive attitude to make full use of all initiatives and resources, and seek various effective methods to guarantee elderly people good living conditions, enhanced medical treatment, and a comfortable retirement.

Population Increment

When the People's Republic of China was founded in 1949, the population numbered 541.67 million. Owing to China's stable society, rapid development of production, improvement in medical and health conditions, insufficient awareness of the importance of population growth control, as well as shortage of experience, the population grew rapidly, reaching 806.71 million in 1969. Since the 1970s, China has implemented a policy of family planning to control population growth, which has brought about a decline in birth rate. By 2007, the annual rate of population growth had decreased to 12.10 per 1,000. Now China's population reproduction picture has basically been turned around, into one characterized by low rates of birth, death and growth.

A couple with one child

Retirees enjoying themselves by playing musical instruments

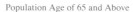
Population Age of 65 and Above

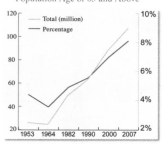

In line with the "Outline of the Eleventh Five-Year Plan (2006-2010) for National Economic and Social Development," adopted at the Fourth Session of the Tenth NPC in March 2006, the annual natural increase of China's population should be kept under 8 per 1,000, so as to ensure the population not to exceed 1.36 billion by 2010.

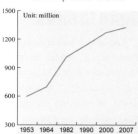

Total Population Growth

Main Regions of Population Migration

Ethnic Groups

Sketch Map Showing Distribution of Ethnic Groups

China is a unitary multi-ethnic nation made up of 56 different ethnic peoples. Because the Han accounts for 91.6% of the population, the other 55 are customarily referred to as "ethnic minorities." According to the fifth national census in 2000, 18 minority peoples have populations of over one million, namely the Zhuang, Manchu, Hui, Miao, Uygur, Yi, Tujia, Mongol, Tibetan, Bouyei, Dong, Yao, Korean, Bai, Hani, Li, Kazak, and Dai; of these, the Zhuang has the biggest population, numbering 16.179 million. There are 17 groups with a population of between 100,000 and one million, namely the She, Lisu, Gelao, Lahu, Dongxiang, Va, Sui, Naxi, Qiang, Tu, Xibe, Mulam, Kirgiz, Daur, Jingpo, Salar, and Maonan. The other 20 minority populations number between 10,000 and 100,000, namely, the Blang, Tajik, Primi, Achang, Nu, Ewenki, Jing, Jino, Deang, Uzbek, Russian, Yugur, Bonan, Monba, Oroqen, Derung, Tatar, Hezhen, Gaoshan (excluding the Gaoshan population in Taiwan), and Lhoba. The Lhoba community has the smallest population, only 2,965.

Uyghur

Tibetan

Ethnic group	Population		Ethnic group	Population		Ethnic group	Population
Han	1.16 b.		Gelao	0.579 m.		Jing	23,000
Mongol	5.814 m.		Xibe	0.189 m		Tatar	5,000
Hui	9.817 m.		Achang	34,000		Derung	7,000
Tibetan	5.416 m.		Primi	34,000		Oroqen	8,000
Uyghur	8.399 m.		Tajik	41,000		Hezhen	5,000
Miao	8.94 m.		Nu	29,000		Monba	9,000
Yi	7.762 m.		Uzbek	12,000		Lhoba	2,965
Zhuang	16.179 m.		Russian	16,000		Jino	21,000
Bouyei	2.971 m.		Ewenki	31,000		Kirgiz	0.161 m.
Korean	1.924 m.		Deang	18,000		Tu	0.241 m.
Manchu	10.682 m.		Boan	17,000		Daur	0.132 m.
Dong	2.96 m.		Yugur	14,000		Mulam	0.207 m.
Yao	2.637 m.		Naxi	0.309 m.		Qiang	0.306 m.
Bai	1.858 m.		Jingpo	0.132 m.		Blang	92,000
Tujia	8.028 m.		Va	0.397 m.		Salar	0.105 m.
Hani	1.44 m.		She	0.710 m.		Maonan	0.107 m.
Kazak	1.25 m.		Gaoshan	4,000		Lisu	0.635 m.
Dai	1.159 m.		Lahu	0.45 m.		Dongxiang	0.514 m.
Li	1.248 m.		Sui	0.407 m.			

Based on the Fifth National Population Census

Hui

Mongol

Harbin

Changchun

Shenyang

Hohhot

Beijing

Yinchuan

Tianjin

Shijiazhuang

Taiyuan

Xining

Jinan

Lanzhou

Zhengzhou

Xi'an

Nanjing

Hefei

Shanghai

Wuhan

Hangzhou

Chengdu

Chongqing

Nanchang

Changsha

Guiyang

Fuzhou

Taibei

Kunming

Guangzhou

Nanning

Macao Hong Kong

Haikou

Manchu

Han

Gaoshan

Zhuang

Books written in Dongba characters of
Naxi Ethnic Minority

The Only Living Pictographs – Dongba Writing

Dongba writing is the ancient language of Naxi people, with a history of over 1,000 years. Originally carved on wood and stone, later it was written down on paper and became a language for writing. Controlled by Dongba flamen, the writing is also called Dongba. It has about 1,400 characters, and is still used by the Naxi Dongba people. It is the only living pictograph language in the world, known as a "living fossil" in the study on human society, and origin and development of characters.

Holidays of Gregorian Calendar

New Year (January 1), International Working Women's Day (March 8), Tree Planting Day (March 12), International Labor Day (May 1), Chinese Youth Day (May 4), International Children's Day (June 1), Anniversary of the Founding of the Chinese People's Liberation Army (August 1), Teacher's Day (September 10), and National Day (October 1).

Spoken and Written Languages

Chinese is the most commonly used language in China, and *han zi* (Chinese written characters) is the most commonly used writing language. All of China's 55 minority peoples have their own languages, except the Hui and the Manchu who only use Chinese; 22 of them have their own scripts, with 28 scripts in total. Nowadays, schools mainly open to minority students all use textbooks compiled in the languages of the minority peoples, while also having courses to teach Chinese characters and *Putonghua*, the national language.

Written Chinese characters originated from a pictographic system invented by Chinese people 4,000 years ago, making it the world's oldest pictographic writing surviving in use until now.

Chinese characters include simplified Chinese characters, popular in China's mainland and Chinese communities in Southeast Asia; as well as traditional Chinese characters, popular in Hong Kong, Macao, Taiwan Province and among overseas Chinese in North America. In recent years, the usage of simplified Chinese characters has grown wider, as more and more people in other countries are choosing Chinese to study as a second language.

Zhonghua Zihai (*Grand Dictionary of Chinese Characters*), published in 1994, gathers more than 85,000 Chinese written characters. The official *Xiandai Hanyu Changyong Zibiao* (*List of Frequently Used Characters in Modern Chinese*), promulgated in 1988, selected a total of 3,500 characters including the 2,500 most frequently used characters and 1,000 in less use.

Traditional Festivals

China's major traditional festivals include the Spring Festival, the Lantern Festival, the Qingming (Pure Brightness) Festival, the Dragon-boat Festival, and the Mid-Autumn Festival. The ethnic minorities have also retained their own traditional festivals, including the Ramadan of the Hui people, the Kurban of the Uygur people, the Water Sprinkling Festival of the Dai people, the Mongolian Nadam Fair, the Torch Festival of the Yi people, the Danu (Never Forget the Past) Festival of the Yao, the Third Month Fair of the Bai people, the Antiphonal Singing Day of the Zhuang, the Tibetan New Year and Ongkor (Expecting a Good Harvest) Festival, and the Jumping Flower Festival of the Miao people.

Spring Festival

In old times when the lunar calendar was used, the Spring Festival was the first day of the first lunar month, the beginning of a new year. After the Revolution of 1911, China adopted the Gregorian calendar. To distinguish the lunar New Year's Day from that of the Gregorian calendar, the former came to be called "Spring Festival," which generally falls between the last 10 days of January and mid-February. The Eve of Spring Festival is an important time for family reunion, when many people stay up all night, "seeing the old year out." During Spring Festival, various traditional activities are enjoyed, notably lion dances, dragon lantern dances, land-boat rowing and stilt-walking.

Spring Festival

Lantern Festival

The Lantern Festival falls on the 15th day of the first lunar month, the first full-moon night after the Spring Festival. Traditionally, people eat *yuanxiao* (sweet dumplings) and admire lanterns on this day. The *yuanxiao*, round balls of glutinous rice flour with sweet filling, symbolizes reunion. The tradition of admiring lanterns emerged in the first century, and is still popular across the country.

Lantern Festival

Pure Brightness Festival

The Qingming or Pure Brightness Festival falls around April 5 every year. Traditionally, this is an occasion for people to make ceremonial offerings to their ancestors. It is also the time to pay respect to revolutionary martyrs. At this time of the year, the weather begins to turn warm, vegetation is bursting into new life and people love to take outings, fly kites and enjoy the beauty of spring. That is why the festival is also called "Spring Outing Day."

Pure Brightness Festival

Dragon-boat Festival

This festival falls on the fifth day of the fifth lunar month, when the weather is turning warm, accompanied by reviving insects. The objective is to kill insects and prevent disease. It is also said that this festival is celebrated to honor the patriotic poet Qu Yuan (c. 340-278 BC) of the State of Chu during the Warring States Period. Failing to realize his political ideals and hold back the decline of his state, Qu Yuan drowned himself in despair in the Miluo River, on the fifth day of the fifth lunar month. Every year thereafter, on this day people would boat on rivers and throw bamboo tubes filled with rice into the water. Today, the memory of Qu Yuan lives on, as *zongzi* (pyramid-shaped-wrapped glutinous rice in bamboo or reed leaves) remains the traditional food, and dragon-boat races are held.

Dragon-boat Festival

Mid-Autumn Festival

The Mid-Autumn Festival falls on the 15th day of the eighth lunar month, which comes right in the middle of autumn. In ancient times, people would offer pastries, or "moon-cakes" as sacrifices to the Moon Goddess on this day. After the ceremony, the family would sit together to share the "moon-cakes." The festival came to symbolize family reunion, as did the "moon-cakes," and the custom has been passed down to today.

Mid-autumn Festival

New Year blessings

Religion

China is a country of great religious diversity, with over 100 million followers of various faiths, more than 100,000 sites for religious activities, about 300,000 religious personnel and over 3,000 religious associations. These associations operate 76 religious schools and colleges to train religious personnel. The main religions are Buddhism, Islam, and Roman Catholic and Protestant Christianity, along with China's indigenous Taoism, Shamanism, Eastern Orthodox Christianity, and the Naxi people's Dongba religion.

China pursues a free religious-belief policy. In China, regular religious activities — such as worshipping Buddha, chanting scriptures, praying, expounding on scriptures, holding Mass, baptism, ordination as monks or nuns, and observance of religious festivals such as Ramadan — are all managed by religious personnel and adherents themselves, and protected by the law and free from interference. The holy books of each religion are published and distributed by religious associations. Each religion has its own national periodical, which is also circulated abroad.

Religious ceremony of consecrating a newly completed Buddha statue at Mt. Lingshan, Wuxi, Jiangsu Province

Taiqing Palace is a Taoist temple on Mount Laoshan, Shandong Province.

Five Main Religions

Buddhism was introduced into China from India around the first century AD, and became the most influential religion in China after the fourth century. Tibetan Buddhism, as a branch of Chinese Buddhism, is popular primarily in Tibet and Inner Mongolia. Now China has more than 13,000 Buddhist temples.

It is probable that Islam first reached China around the mid-seventh century. The Yuan Dynasty witnessed the zenith of the prosperity of Islam in the country. Now China has more than 30,000 mosques.

Catholic influence reached China in the seventh century. Now there are more than 4,600 Catholic churches in China.

Protestantism was introduced into China in the early 19th century. There are over 12,000 Protestant churches, in addition to 30,000 temporary places of worship.

Taoism is based on the philosophy of Lao Zi (traditionally said to be born in 604 BC) and his work *Dao De Jing* (*Classic of the Way and Virtue*). It probably took shape as a religion during the second century. China now has more than 1,500 Taoist temples.

A mosque in Yinchuan, Ningxia   A Catholic church in Beijing   Christians receiving the baptism

Political System
and State Structure

The Constitution

Since the founding of the People's Republic of China in 1949, four Constitutions have been formulated successively, in 1954, 1975, 1978 and 1982. The present 1982 Constitution contains 138 articles. Amendments to the Constitution have been made four times, the last time being in 2004. The Constitution stipulates that all citizens are equal before the law and that the state respects and safeguards human rights. It guarantees the basic rights and interests of citizens, including the right to vote and stand for election; freedom of speech, of the press, of assembly, of association, of procession and of demonstration; freedom of religious belief; the inviolability of the freedom of the person, personal dignity, residence and legitimate private property; freedom and privacy of correspondence; the right to criticize and make suggestions to any state organ or functionary, and exercise supervision; the right to work and rest, and the right to material assistance from the state and society when old, ill or disabled; and the right to receive education, and freedom to engage in scientific research, literary and artistic creation, and other cultural pursuits.

Four Amendments to the Current Constitution

The 1988 amendment to the Constitution stipulates that, the State permits the private sector of the economy to exist and develop within the limits prescribed by law, and the right to the use of lands may be transferred according to law. The 1993 amendment to the Constitution stipulates that, the State practices a socialist market economy, and the system of multi-party cooperation and political consultation under the leadership of the CPC will exist and develop for a long time. The 1999 amendment to the Constitution stipulates that, the State governs the country by law, and adheres to the basic economic system with public ownership playing the dominant role alongside developing diverse forms of ownership. The 2004 amendment to the Constitution stipulates that, citizens' legal private property should not be infringed upon, with the State guaranteeing citizens' private property and rights of inheritance according to law; and the State respects and protects human rights.

Political System

The basic structure of China's political system consists of the leadership of the CPC, the people's congress system, the multiparty cooperation and political consultation system, and the regional ethnic autonomy system.

Legal System

China's legal system consists of seven categories: Constitution and related laws, civil and commercial laws, administrative laws, economic laws, social laws, criminal laws, and litigation and non-litigation procedural laws. By the end of 2007, more than 500 laws and law-related decisions had been made by the NPC and its Standing Committee, over 1,000 administrative regulations had been made by the State Council, and more than 10,000 local regulations made by local people's congresses, covering political, economic and social fields. A relatively complete legal system is now basically in place.

The Great Hall of the People — China's parliament building

The People's Congress System

In China, the organs through which the people exercise state power are the National People's Congress (NPC) and local people's congresses. Therefore, the people's congress system is China's fundamental political system. Its basic feature is adherence to the principle of democratic centralism, i.e., the people enjoy extensive democracy and rights, while at the same time state power is exercised in a centralized and unified way. Under the premise that the people's congresses exercise state power in a unified way, the state's administrative power, judicial authority, procuratorial authority and leadership over the armed forces are clearly divided, so as to ensure that the organs of state power and administrative, judicial, procuratorial and other state organs work in a coordinated way.

An ethnic minority delegate taking a vote

Deputies to the people's congresses at all levels are elected. They include people from all ethnic groups, all walks of life, and all regions, classes and strata. When the congresses meet, they can air their views fully; they can also address inquiries to governments at the corresponding level and their affiliated departments, and the parties concerned are duty-bound to reply to the inquiries. Electors or constituencies have the right to recall their elected deputies according to procedures prescribed by law.

Multiparty Cooperation and Political Consultation System

China is a country that is multiethnic and with multiple political parties. Before the state adopts important measures or makes decisions on major issues with a bearing on the national economy and the people's livelihood, the CPC, as the party in power, consults with representatives of all political parties, as well as democrats without party affiliation. This system of multiparty cooperation and political consultation led by the CPC is the basic political system in China.

Multiparty cooperation and political consultation take two principal forms: (1) Chinese People's Political Consultative Conference (CPPCC); (2) consultative conferences and forums with the participation of people from Democratic Parties (non-Communist parties) and people without party affiliation, at the invitation of the CPC. The CPPCC National Committee consists of representatives of the CPC, non-Communist parties, people without party affiliation, people's organizations, ethic minorities, and other social strata, and specially invited individuals. The CPPCC is elected for a term of five years. In addition to attending a plenary session of the CPPCC once a year, CPPCC National Committee members are invited to attend the NPC and fully air their views as non-voting delegates, so as to exercise the functions of political consultation, democratic supervision and participation in the deliberation and administration of state affairs. Once a year, leaders of the CPC Central Committee invite leaders of the non-Communist parties and representatives of people without party affiliation to consultation meetings; forums are held every other month. The former focuses on major state policies, the latter on exchange of information, receiving policy proposals and discussing special issues. The current Chairman of the CPPCC is Jia Qinglin.

Regional Ethnic Autonomy System

China practices a regional ethnic autonomy system. Where minorities live in compact communities, organs of self-government are established under the unified leadership of the state. Minority peoples exercise autonomous rights, are masters in their own areas, and administer their own internal affairs. The Central Government also actively aids the ethnic autonomous areas with funds and materials, so as to promote the development of their local economies and cultures. The Law on Regional Ethnic Autonomy, adopted in 1984 at the Second Session of the Sixth NPC, is the basic law guaranteeing the implementation of the regional ethnic autonomy system. Today, in addition to the five autonomous regions (Inner Mongolia, Xinjiang Uygur, Guangxi Zhuang, Ningxia Hui and Tibet autonomous regions), China has 30 autonomous prefectures and 120 autonomous counties (banners), as well as over 1,100 ethnic townships. The organs of self-government in ethnic autonomous areas are the people's congresses and people's governments of autonomous regions, autonomous prefectures, and autonomous counties (banners). The chairperson or vice-chairs of the standing committee of the people's congress and the head of an autonomous region, autonomous prefecture or autonomous county (banner) should be citizens of the community exercising regional autonomy in the area concerned.

Organs of self-government in ethnic autonomous areas enjoy extensive self-government rights beyond those held by other state organs at the same level. These include: enacting regulations on the exercise of autonomy and separate regulations corresponding to the political, economic and cultural characteristics of the ethnic group(s) in the areas concerned; having the freedom to manage and use all revenues accruing to the ethnic autonomous areas; independently arranging and managing local economic development, education, science, culture, public health and physical culture, protecting and organizing their cultural heritage, and developing and invigorating their cultures.

National People's Congress

The NPC, the highest organ of state power, consists of deputies elected by all the provinces, autonomous regions, municipalities directly under the Central Government, special administrative regions, and the armed forces. It exercises legislative power and makes decisions on important issues regarding national political life. Its main functions and powers include: enacting and amending laws; examining and approving national economic and social development plans, state budgets and reports on their implementation; making decisions on matters of war and peace; electing and choosing the leadership of the highest organs of state, i.e., electing the members of the Standing Committee of the NPC, the state President, the Premier of the State Council, and the Chairman of the Central Military Commission, with the power to recall any of the above mentioned. The NPC is elected for a term of five years, and is now at its 11th term. The current Chairman of the Standing Committee of the NPC is Wu Bangguo.

National People's Congress

Standing Committee of the NPC

General Office

Special Committees
Ethnic Affairs Committee
Legal Committee
Internal and Judicial Affairs Committee
Financial and Economic Affairs Committee
Education, Science, Culture and Public Health Committee
Foreign Affairs Committee
Overseas Chinese Affairs Committee
Environmental Protection and Resources Conservation Committee
Agriculture and Rural Affairs Committee

Working and Administrative Bodies
Legislative Affairs Commission
Budgetary Affairs Commission
Hong Kong Special Administrative Region Basic Law Committee
Macao Special Administrative Region Basic Law Committee

Local People's Congresses

On March 5, the First Session of the 11th National People's Congress of People's Republic of China was held in Beijing.

Presidency

Working together with the NPC Standing Committee, the President of the PRC exercises his or her functions and powers as the head of state. The President, pursuant to decisions of the NPC or its Standing Committee, promulgates laws, appoints and removes members of the State Council, and issues orders; on behalf of the PRC, conducts state activities, receives foreign diplomatic representatives, dispatches and recalls plenipotentiary representatives abroad, and ratifies or abrogates treaties and important agreements reached with foreign states. The current President is Hu Jintao.

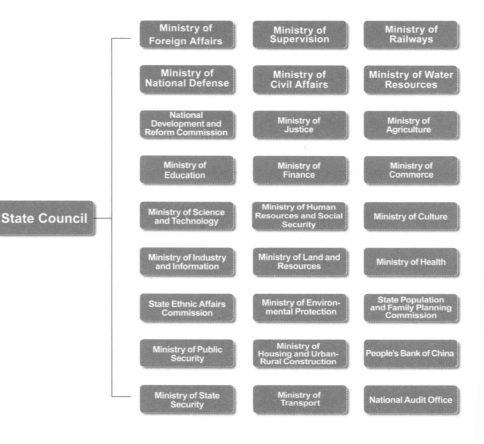

State Council

The State Council is the Central People's Government. It is the executive body of the highest organ of state power (the NPC), and also the highest state administrative body. The State Council is responsible to the NPC and its Standing Committee, and reports to them on its work. The State Council has the power to formulate administrative measures, enact administrative regulations, and promulgate decisions and orders within its functions and powers. The State Council is composed of the premier, the vice-premiers, the state councilors, the secretary-general, the ministers in charge of ministries, the ministers in charge of commissions, the governor of the People's Bank of China, and the auditor-general of the National Audit Office. The current premier is Wen Jiabao.

Central Military Commission

The Central Military Commission is the nation's leading military organ and commander of its armed forces. China's armed forces consist of the Chinese People's Liberation Army (PLA), the Chinese People's Armed Police Force, and the Militia. The PLA is the standing army of the state. The main tasks of the Armed Police Force include performing guard duties and maintaining public order, as empowered by the state. The Militia is an armed force of the masses and, when not on duty, remains engaged in their normal productive activities. The Central Military Commission is composed of the chair, vice-chairs and other members. The current Chairman is Hu Jintao.

Local People's Congresses and Local People's Governments

Reflecting existing national administrative divisions, there are people's congresses and people's governments at all levels – in provinces, autonomous regions and municipalities directly under the Central Government; in cities (autonomous prefectures and autonomous leagues); in counties (autonomous counties and autonomous banners); in townships and towns. The people's congresses at and above the county level have standing committees.

The local people's congresses are the local organs of state power. They have the power to decide on important affairs in their respective administrative areas. The people's congresses of provinces, autonomous regions and municipalities directly under the Central Government have the power to formulate local regulations. Local people's governments are the local administrative organs. Working under the unified leadership of the State Council, they are responsible to and report on their work to the people's congresses and their standing committees at the corresponding level and to the organs of state administration at the next higher level. They have overall responsibility for the administrative work within their respective administrative areas.

People's Courts

The people's courts are the judicial organs of the state. The Supreme People's Court is established at the state level; higher people's courts are established in provinces, autonomous regions and municipalities directly under the Central Government; and intermediate and grassroots people's courts at lower levels. The Supreme People's Court, the state's highest judicial organ, reports to the NPC and its Standing Committee, and supervises the judicial work of the local people's courts, military courts and other special courts. The current president of the Supreme People's Court is Wang Shengjun.

People's Procuratorates

The people's procuratorates are state organs of legal supervision. Their organization corresponds to that of the people's courts. The people's procuratorates have the right to exercise procuratorial authority. They exercise this authority over cases endangering state and public security, damaging economic order and infringing on citizens' personal and democratic rights, as well as over other important criminal cases; examine cases scheduled for investigation by public security agencies, and decide on whether suspects should s Cao Jianming.

The Relationship Between the NPC, the CPPCC and the State Council

The National People's Congress (NPC) exercises power through election, ballot and voting, fully consulting the Chinese People's Political Consultative Conference (CPPCC) before elections and voting. These are the two most important manifestations of China's socialist democracy. The relationship between the NPC, the CPPCC and the State Council is that, the CPPCC will be consulted before policymaking, after which the NPC votes on policymaking, and the State Council is responsible for policy implementation. They fulfill their separate duties with full cooperation and mutual reliance, while complementing each other under the unified leadership of the CPC. This political system with Chinese characteristics suits China's conditions.

Chinese People's Political Consultative Conference

The Chinese People's Political Consultative Conference (CPPCC) is an organization of the Chinese people's patriotic united front as well as an important institution of multi-party cooperation and political consultation under the leadership of the CPC. Moreover, it is also an important channel to promote socialist democracy in China's political life.

The main functions of the CPPCC are political consultation, democratic supervision, and participation in the deliberation and administration of state affairs.

The CPPCC has the National Committee and local committees.

CPPCC National Committee

The CPPCC National Committee consists of the CPC, non-Communist parties, people without party affiliation, people's organizations, ethnic minorities, and other social strata, representatives of the Hong Kong and Macao special administrative regions, Taiwan Province and returned overseas Chinese, and specially invited individuals.

The CPPCC National Committee is elected for a term of five years, and is now at its 11th term.

The Chairman of the 11th CPPCC National Committee is Jia Qinglin.

Local Committees of the CPPCC

The committees of CPPCC have been set up in all provinces, autonomous regions, municipalities directly under the Central Government, autonomous prefectures, cities with districts, counties, autonomous counties, cities without districts, and municipal districts.

National Committee of the CPPCC

Standing Committee of the National Committee of the CPPCC

Special Committees
Committee for Handling Proposals
Committee for Economic Affairs
Committee on Population, Resources and Environment
Committee on Education, Science, Culture, Health and Sports
Committee for Social and Legal Affairs
Committee for Ethnic and Religious Affairs
Committee for Liaison with Hong Kong, Macao, Taiwan and
   Overseas Chinese
Committee for Foreign Affairs
Committee for Cultural and Historical Study

Local CPPCC Committees

Political Parties and Other Organizations

Communist Party of China

Founded in July 1921, the Communist Party of China (CPC) today has 73.36 million members.

From 1921 to 1949, the CPC led the Chinese people in their arduous struggle that finally brought about the expelling of Japanese aggressors and the establishment of the People's Republic of China (PRC). After the founding of the PRC, the CPC led the Chinese people in carrying out systematic large-scale socialist construction. The CPC's lack of experience led to some errors in leading the process of constructing socialism, followed by the serious mistake of launching the "cultural revolution" (1966-1976).

The "cultural revolution" ended in October 1976, at which turning point China entered a new historic era of development. Following the Third Plenary Session of the 11th CPC Central Committee at the end of 1978, the country embarked on the biggest change

Xinhua Gate of Zhongnanhai, where the CPC Central Committee locates

in the history of New China. Since then, China's economic and social development has been crowned with remarkable success.

The highest leading organ of the CPC is the National Congress, which is held once every five years. When the National Congress is not in session, the Central Committee implements decisions made by the National Congress and leads all work of the Party. From October 15 to 21, 2007, the CPC held the 17th National Congress, reviewing and summarizing the historical course and valuable experience of China's reform and opening-up, and putting forward major policies and specific goals for the new period. It also amended the Party Constitution and elected the new Central Committee members. The current General Secretary of the Central Committee is Hu Jintao.

Governing Concepts

The core of the governing concepts of the Communist Party of China (CPC) is maintaining a people-oriented concept and wholehearted service to the people.

The governing concept of the CPC: We should build a party for the public interest and exercise governance for the people; exercise government power in a scientific, democratic and law-based manner, becoming a ruling party that is realistic, pragmatic and hardworking, yet effective, open, clean and committed to reform and innovation; and lead all the Chinese people to strive toward the country's prosperity, national rejuvenation, social harmony and the well-being of all.

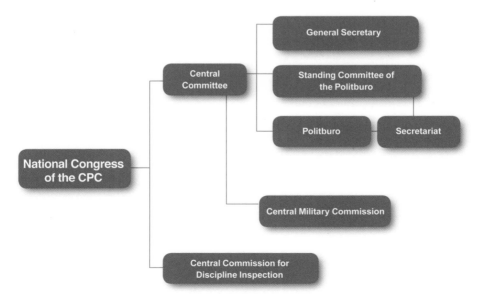

Democratic Parties

Besides the CPC, China has eight other political parties. These parties all support the CPC's political leadership, and enjoy political freedom, organizational independence and lawful equality within the vested scope of the Constitution. The basic principle of the cooperation between the CPC and the other parties is long-term coexistence, mutual supervision, sincere treatment of each other, and sharing each other's successes and failures.

Many of their members hold posts in the standing committees of

On March 6, 2008, the First Session of the 11th Chinese People's Political Consultative Conference held press conference. Chairpersons of eight democratic parties made their debut.

The Eight Democratic Parties

Revolutionary Committee of the Chinese Kuomintang
Established in January 1948
Former members of the KMT and people having historical connections with the KMT
Chairperson: Zhou Tienong

China Democratic League
Established in October 1941
Higher and mid-level intellectuals
Chairperson: Jiang Shusheng

China Democratic National Construction Association
Established in December 1945
Specialists, scholars and other people in the economic field
Chairperson: Chen Changzhi

China Association for Promoting Democracy
Established in December 1945
Intellectuals working in educational, cultural, scientific, publishing and other fields
Chairperson: Yan Juanqi

Chinese Peasants and Workers Democratic Party
Established in August 1930
Higher and mid-level intellectuals in the fields of medicine, culture, education, and science and technology
Chairperson: Sang Guowei

China Zhi Gong Dang
Established in October 1925
Returned overseas Chinese, relatives of overseas Chinese, representative individuals, specialists, and scholars with overseas connections
Chairperson: Wan Gang

Jiusan Society
Established in December 1944
Higher and mid-level intellectuals working in fields of science and technology, culture, education and public health
Chairperson: Han Qide

Taiwan Democratic Self-government League
Established in November 1947
People born or with family roots in Taiwan Province currently residing on the mainland
Chairperson: Lin Wenyi

the people's congresses, CPPCC committees, government organs, and economic, cultural, educational, scientific and technological departments. For instance, the chairpersons of the eight parties' central committees are concurrently vice-chairs of the NPC Standing Committee or the CPPCC National Committee. With a combined number of members exceeding 700,000, they have set up branches and grassroots organizations in all the provinces, autonomous regions and municipalities directly under the Central Government, and in large and medium cities.

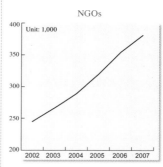

Mass Organizations and NGOs

Chinese mass organizations carry out their activities independently in accordance with the Constitution and the law. Their branches cover urban and rural areas, participate in national and local political life, and play an important role in coordinating social and public affairs and safeguarding the legitimate rights and interests of the people.

According to statistics from the Ministry of Civil Affairs, there were only 446 NGOs in China in 1989. By the end of 2007, China had 381,000 NGOs, including 207,000 mass organizations, 172,000 community-run non-business organizations, and 1,369 foundations.

Chinese NGOs are mainly engaged in technology, education, culture, hygiene, sports, environmental protection, legal services, and intermediary social services. NGOs work together with the government to promote environmental protection, which is an important characteristic and new trend in the field of environmental protection. Environmental-protection NGOs have become an important force in popularizing environmental education and promoting public participation.

Major Mass Organizations

All-China Federation of Trade Unions	**All-China Youth Federation**	**All-China Women's Federation**	**All-China Federation of Industry and Commerce**
Established in May 1925 Workers Chairman: Wang Zhaoguo	*Established in May 1949* Youth from all walks of life First Secretary: Yang Yue	*Established in April 1949* Women from all walks of life Chairwoman: Gu Xiulian	*Established in October 1953* People in the non-public economic sectors Chairman: Huang Mengfu

The People's Army

Percentage of National Defense Spending in Total Financial Expenditure

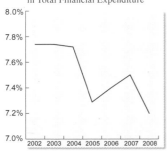

Percentage of Major Countries' National Defense Spending in GDP in 2007

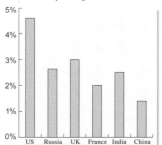

China follows a national defense policy that is defensive in nature. China's national defense is a crucial guarantee for its national existence, development, security and unity, and for the goal of achieving the building of a moderately prosperous society in all respects. It is a strategic task for the country to build a strong and powerful national defense.

The policies of China's national defense include maintaining national security and unity; guaranteeing the interests of national development; achieving all-round coordinated and sustainable development of national defense and army building; strengthening the quality of army building, characterized by the full application of technical informatization; implementing the military strategic principle of active defense; adhering to a nuclear strategy of self-defense; and building a safe environment for peaceful national development.

The armed forces of the People's Republic of China consist of the People's Liberation Army (PLA), the Chinese People's Armed Police Force and People's Militias, under the unified leadership of the Central Military Commission.

The PLA, which consists of active army and inactive units, is the main body of China's armed forces, with total personnel of less than 2.3 million.

The Chinese People's Armed Police Force undertakes the responsibility of maintaining national security and social stability, safeguarding significant state targets and guaranteeing the safety of people's lives and property. During wartime, it will assist the PLA in defense work.

People's Militias are people's armed organizations, which are not divorced from production. During peacetime, they undertake the responsibility of being on duty for war readiness, rescue and relief work and maintenance of social order. In wartime, they will fight in cooperation with the standing army, as well as fight independently, offering combat and supplementary services to the standing army, etc.

Honor guard of the PLA

China and the World

Foreign Policy

China pursues an independent foreign policy of peace, with the fundamental objectives being to maintain world peace, promote common development, and contribute to the building of a harmonious world of lasting peace and common prosperity. Its main elements are as follows:

— Unswervingly following the path of peaceful development. China maintains that all countries, big and small, strong and weak, rich and poor, are equal. China respects the right of the people of all countries to independently choose their own development path. No country shall interfere in the internal affairs of other countries or impose its own will on others.

— Working for the promotion of international and regional security cooperation. China opposes all forms of hegemonism and power politics, and will never seek hegemony or engage in expansion.

— Developing friendship and cooperation with all other countries on the basis of the "Five Principles of Peaceful Coexistence." Toward developed countries, China continues to strengthen strategic dialogue, enhance mutual trust, deepen cooperation and appropriately manage differences, to promote long-term, stable and sound development of bilateral relations. Toward neighboring countries, China continues to follow the foreign policy of friendship and partnership, strengthening good-neighborly relations and practical cooperation, and actively engaging in regional cooperation, so as to jointly create a peaceful, stable regional environment focused on equality, mutual trust and win-win cooperation. With other developing countries, China continues to increase solidarity and cooperation, reinforce traditional friendship, expand practical cooperation, provide assistance within our ability, and uphold the legitimate demands and common interests of developing countries. China takes an active part in multilateral affairs, assumes its due international obligations, plays a constructive role, and works to make the international order fairer and more equitable.

Principles for Establishing Diplomatic Relations

There is only one China in the world. Taiwan is an inalienable part of China's territory. Any nation that intends to have diplomatic relations with China must recognize the PRC government as the sole legitimate government of China, and be willing to observe the principles of mutual respect for territorial integrity and sovereignty, mutual non-aggression, non-interference in each other's internal affairs, equality and mutual benefit, and peaceful coexistence.

In line with these principles, China had established diplomatic relations with 171 countries by the end of 2007.

Relations with Neighboring Countries

China pursues a policy of friendship and partnership with neighboring countries and a policy of enhancing harmony, security and prosperity. It works with them to jointly create a peaceful, stable regional environment based on equality, mutual trust and win-win cooperation.

In 2007, President Hu Jintao of the PRC visited Kyrgyzstan

and Kazakhstan, while the State Council's Premier Wen Jiabao visited Uzbekistan and Turkmenistan, further strengthening China's relations with Central Asian countries. Premier Wen Jiabao successively attended the 10th ASEAN-China, Japan and ROK (10+3) Summit, the 10th China-ASEAN (10+1) Summit, and the Second East Asia Summit, the 11th ASEAN-China, Japan and ROK (10+3) Summit, the 11th China-ASEAN (10+1) Summit, the 3rd East Asia Summit and the 8th China, Japan and Korea Summit; among others. At these conferences, Premier Wen put forward numerous detailed proposals for cooperation, covering such fields as politics, security, economy and trade, environment, sustainable development, and culture. During Indian Prime Minister Manmohan Singh's visit to China in January of 2008, India and China reached a broad agreement on further deepening of strategic cooperative partnership, under the new situation, bringing a new drive for comprehensive bilateral cooperation.

In 2007, China attended the Summit of the South Asian Association for Regional Cooperation (SAARC) for the first time, with observer status, enhancing its relations with SAARC and taking them to a new stage. It also accelerated its dialogue with ASEAN on the Agreement on Services and the Agreement on Investment, laying a solid foundation for the scheduled establishment of the China-ASEAN Free Trade Zone.

President Hu Jintao attending a summit with leaders from four developing countries, India, Brazil, South Africa and Mexico, in Berlin, June 7, 2007.

Relations with Developing Countries

As the world's largest developing country, China takes consolidating and developing cooperation with other developing countries as a cornerstone of its foreign policy. In 2007, China continued strengthening friendship and cooperation with developing countries, and gave prominence to the fundamental role of relations with developing countries, trying to build up a new-type partnership based on long-term stability, equality and mutual benefit, as well as all-round cooperation.

In 2007, President Hu Jintao, Chairman Wu Bangguo of the Standing Committee of the NPC and Chairman Jia Qinglin of the CPPCC successively visited Africa; Premier Wen Jiabao attended the annual meeting of the African Development Bank (AFDB), pushing forward the implementation of the fruits reaped at the Beijing Summit of the Forum on China-Africa Cooperation, especially the eight "Africa-targeted Measures." Foreign ministers of China and African countries held their first political consultation during the General Assembly of the United Nations, formally launching a regular Sino-African dialogue mechanism at the foreign-ministerial level, under the framework of the Forum on China-Africa Cooperation. In

May, China successfully launched a communication satellite for Nigeria, making it the first African country to independently own a satellite. From July, the 26 least-developed countries in Africa have enjoyed zero-tariff treatment for their 454 exports into China. China has also sent nearly 1,300 personnel to take part in seven UN peace-keeping missions in Africa.

In 2007, the Second Entrepreneurs' Conference of the China-Arab Cooperation Forum was successfully held. China has been taking an active part in resolving the Iran nuclear issue. It also made positive and effective efforts toward resolving the Darfur issue, appointing a special representative for African affairs. In 2007, China strengthened mutual political trust with Latin American countries; developed economic and trade cooperation; and made new achievements in cooperation in the fields of culture, education, science and technology. China also strengthened coordination and cooperation with rising major developing countries, including India, Brazil, South Africa, and Mexico.

Relations with Major Countries

China adheres to the policy of expanding common interest with the world's major powers, and resolving differences in a proper way, based on the "Five Principles of Peaceful Coexistence."

Sino-US Relations

In 2007, Sino-US relations moved steadily forward. Leaders of the two countries maintained close communication and contact. President Hu Jintao met President George W. Bush in June, when G8 leaders conferred with leaders of six developing countries, and in September during the Informal APEC Leadership Meeting. The two leaders have often exchanged views by mail or phone in a timely manner on bilateral relations and important international or regional issues. In November, US Defense Secretary Robert M. Gates visited China, and the two sides reached several consensuses regarding the promotion of exchange and mutual trust between the military forces of the two countries. Sino-US dialogue and consultation mechanisms at all levels were improved. The two countries held the Fourth Sino-US Strategic Dialogue, followed by the Second and then Third Strategic Economic Dialogue. The NPC of China and the Senate and House of Representatives of the US Congress conducted active institutionalized exchanges. The two countries also maintained close contact through over 50 bilateral working mechanisms, covering politics, economy, military affairs, jurisdiction, science and technology, education, energy, aviation, and climate change. Economic and trade cooperation between China and the US has continued to rapidly develop, as each other's second-largest trade partner.

On April 21, 2006, President Hu Jintao presented Yale University with books from China during his visit to the US. The picture shows President Hu introducing the books to teachers and students of the university.

Sino-Russian Relations

The year 2007 witnessed a highpoint in Sino-Russian relations, with leaders of the two countries having more frequent contacts. The Sino-Russian strategic and cooperative partnership was further consolidated and improved. The leaders of the two countries determined the principles and goals for the second ten-year development of this partnership. In 2007, Russia launched the "Year of China," with President Hu Jintao attending the opening ceremony when visiting Russia in March, while Premier Wen Jiabao attended the closing ceremony and other activities during his visit in November. The China National Exhibition held in Moscow in March was the overseas state-level exhibition of the largest scale and covered the most fields. Sino-Russian military cooperation advanced steadily. In September, troops of the Ministry of Internal Affairs of Russia and the Chinese People's Armed Police Forces carried out a joint counter-terrorism military exercise in the suburbs of Moscow, dubbed "Cooperation 2007." The healthy development of Sino-Russian political relations also contributed to Sino-Russian economic and trade cooperation; the trade structure was remarkably improved, with mutual investment expanding steadily, and the region and range for cooperation constantly expanding.

President Hu Jintao met Russian President Vladimir Putin at the Kremlin, March 2007.

China-EU Relations

The year 2007 saw more frequent communication between leaders of China and the European Union (EU), along with cooperation in additional fields. The cooperation between the two parties became more dimensional, wide-ranging and multilayered, as the all-round strategic China-EU partnership matured. The two sides increased contact and cooperation in world affairs, including the Iran nuclear issue, the situation in the Middle East and the North Korea nuclear issue, and global challenges including climate change and energy issues. The EU has become the No. 1 trade partner of China, as well as the largest export market for China, while China has become the No. 2 trade partner of the EU.

President Hu Jintao met European Commission President José Manuel Barroso in the Great Hall of the People, Beijing, in April 2008.

In early 2007, China and the EU formally launched pragmatic negotiations on a new partnership pact covering all the fields of China-EU relations, including energy, environment, agriculture, transport, customs, education, information society, science and technology, space cooperation, sustainable development, immigration, counter-terrorism, and weapons of mass destruction, laying a comprehensive foundation for the development of China-EU political, economical and trade relations. In July, the Third China-EU Economic and Financial Dialogue was held in Brussels. In October, the Second China-EU Forum was held in Europe. At the end of November, Portuguese Prime Minister Jose Socrates, whose country held the 2007 EU presidency, and European Commission President José Manuel Barroso came to China and attended the Ninth China-EU Summit; and the two sides agreed that China-EU relations

had made historical breakthroughs over the past decade, and reached consensus on problems of mutual concern such as the establishment of a high-level economic and trade dialogue mechanism.

In June, President Hu Jintao attended the meeting of leaders of G8 and developing countries held in Germany, and paid a state visit to Sweden. Spanish King Juan Carlos I, German Chancellor Angela Merkel and French President Nicolas Sarkozy visited China in June, August and November, respectively. These high-level visits between China and European countries upgraded overall relations between China and Europe.

Sino-Japanese Relations

The year 2007 marked the 35th anniversary of the normalization of Sino-Japanese diplomatic relations, as well as the recovery and development of Sino-Japanese relations. In early January, Premier Wen Jiabao met former Japanese Prime Minister Shinzo Abe at the East Asia Summit held in Cebu, the Philippines. In April, Wen visited Japan, which brought official exchanges between China and Japan to a high point. President Hu Jintao met Shinzo Abe at the G8 Summit held in Heiligendamm, Germany, in June, and at the APEC meeting held in Sydney, Australia, in September. During the two meetings, the two sides agreed that they would practically push forward strategic reciprocal relations and strengthen cooperation in the fields of global warming, environmental protection, energy conservation, and the economy. At the end of November, Premier Wen Jiabao met the new Japanese Prime Minister Yasuo Fukuda in Singapore. At the end of December, Yasuo Fukuda visited China and reached an agreement with China on building and developing Sino-Japanese strategic reciprocal relations. China and Japan restored high-level military exchanges, which had been interrupted for ten years. And the two countries also held the China-Japan Culture and Sports Exchange Year and the first high-level economic dialogue themed "cooperation, win-win, and coordinated development."

President Hu Jintao meeting Japanese Prime Minister Yasuo Fukuda in Tokyo, on May 7, 2008

From May 6, 2008, President Hu Jintao conducted a five-day historic state visit to Japan. During his visit, Hu Jintao met Japanese Emperor Akihito, held talks with Japanese Prime Minister Yasuo Fukuda, and had broad contacts with public figures from various circles in Japan. The two sides signed a joint statement on all-round promotion of strategic and mutually beneficial relations between China and Japan. The joint statement formulates the guiding principles for long-term development of bilateral relations, and maps out the future for Sino-Japanese relations.

China and SCO

China continued fostering good-neighborly friendship and cooperation between member states of the Shanghai Cooperation Organization (SCO), pushing forward the development of the Organization's practical cooperation and mechanism-building. In August 2007, the Seventh Meet-

President Hu Jintao attended the inauguration of the China-Japan Youth Friendly Exchange Year, in Beijing, on March 15, 2008. The picture shows President Hu Jintao at a calligraphy exchange activity between Chinese and Japanese youths at Renmin University.

ing of the Council of Heads of SCO Member States was held in Bishkek, capital of Kyrgyzstan; in November, the Sixth Meeting of Prime Ministers of SCO Member States was held in Tashkent, capital of Uzbekistan; and President Hu Jintao attended the Meeting of Heads of States, while Premier Wen Jiabao attended the Prime Ministers' Meeting. During the Bishkek Summit, heads of the six member countries signed the "Treaty on Long-term Good-Neighborliness, Friendship and Cooperation of SCO Members," an important political and legal document outlining criteria for relations between SCO members; the treaty was also a milestone in the SCO history. "Peace Mission 2007," joint counter-terrorism military exercises conducted by armed forces of SCO member states in August, became the largest-scale activity involving the most members since the establishment of the SCO. It strengthened mutual trust of SCO member states in the military and security fields.

China and APEC

China always takes an active part in the activities of the Asia-Pacific Economic Cooperation (APEC), in the spirit of reserving differences while seeking common ground and promoting cooperation. In September 2007, at the 15th APEC Economic Leaders' Informal Meeting in Sydney, Australia, President Hu Jintao delivered several important speeches, elucidating the policies and stance of the Chinese government on critical issues of regional or global interest. He put forward a four-point proposal on economic development and environmental protection: continuing cooperation as indispensable; pursuing sustainable development; upholding the leading position of the UN Framework Convention on Climate Change as the core mechanism in addressing climate change; and promoting scientific and technological innovations. He also proposed to set up the Asia-Pacific Network on Forest Rehabilitation and Sustainable Management. It was the first time that the Chinese government had proposed detailed and practical advice for cooperation at international meetings addressing climate change, and thus it received praise and support from all sides.

China and WTO

Over the six years since its entry into the World Trade Organization (WTO), China has worked hard and actively to fulfill its commitments, and has made progress and remarkable achievements in improving its relevant laws and regulations, transforming its government functions, and making policies more transparent. In 2007, China took an active part in the Doha Talks, with its constructive role gradually attracting attention from all sides. In June, WTO Chief Pascal Lamy visited China, furthering the progress of the Doha Round Talks. On November 27, the WTO formally appointed a Chinese lawyer, Zhang Yuejiao, as member of its Appellate Body, becom-

ing the first in China's mainland to take an important position in the WTO. On November 28, China formally informed the WTO that it had approved the "Protocol Amending the Agreement on Trade-Related Aspects of Intellectual Property Rights (TRIPS)." On December 28, China formally commenced negotiations for membership in the Government Procurement Agreement (GPA).

China has so far solved several trade disputes under the WTO framework. On September 14, China brought to the WTO Dispute Settlement Body (DSB) the case of US anti-dumping and anti-subsidy measures targeting Chinese coated paper, the first time since its entry into the WTO that China independently filed against another member under the WTO's dispute settlement mechanism. On November 29, Sun Zhenyu, Chinese Ambassador and Permanent Representative to the WTO, with Peter Allgeier, US Ambassador and Permanent Representative to the WTO, and Fernando de Mateo y Venturini, Mexican Ambassador and Permanent Representative to the WTO, signed the "Memorandum of Understanding Regarding Certain Measures Granting Refunds, Reductions or Exemptions from Taxes or Other Payments." The subsidy dispute cases between China and the US, and between China and Mexico, were thus concluded.

China and UN

As a permanent member state of the United Nations Security Council, China strives to integrate itself into the international system, to promote multilateralism centering on safeguarding of UN authority, to advocate the establishment of a just and rational international political order, to oppose unilateralism and hegemonism, and to work toward

The Security Council of the United Nations

democratic and law-based world relations. China actively takes part in UN cooperation in peacekeeping, arms control, counter-terrorism, as well as endeavors to foster development, defend human rights and justice, and environmental protection, along with participating in the activities of UN specialized agencies. China also attaches great importance to other multilateral systems, promotes international arms control and disarmament, supports the multilateral arms-control process including the development of non-proliferation mechanisms; it also supports multilateral practical cooperation relating to counter-terrorism, non-proliferation, humanitarian aid, climate and environment, and transnational crime. China takes an active part in UN reforms, toward the objective of the UN giving as much scope as possible to the rational demands and concerns of developing countries.

China's soldiers received UN Peacekeeping Medals.

China's peacekeeping medical team, called "Angels in the Rainforests" by the local people, giving food and medicine to villagers in Libya

In August 2007, Chinese representatives to the UN announced two decisions of the Chinese government in regard to enhancing its transparency on armaments. According to the decisions, from 2007 China would be committed to the UN system of transparency in military expenditure and the UN Register of Conventional Arms, and at the same time, submit "Military Expenditure of China in 2006" and "Data of Conventional Arms Transfer of China in 2006." In December, at the 13th United Nations Framework Convention on Climate Change (UNFCCC) held in Bali Island, Indonesia, China proposed China's National Climate Change Program, which asserts that China will reduce energy consumption per unit GDP by 2010 by 20%, compared with 2005; and raise the proportion of renewable energy in primary energy supply up to 10% by 2010 and to 16% by 2020. China also took an active part in UN peacekeeping activities. It supported UN peacekeeping missions in the Democratic Republic of Congo by sending peacekeeping soldiers, who were later awarded UN peacekeeping medals.

China takes a positive and responsible attitude toward paying its UN membership dues. In 2007, China increased its dues by 40% over 2006, namely, from 2.05% to 2.67%, a larger increase rarely seen among other UN members. This demonstrates China's role as an internationally responsible country.

The Economy

Development

Today, China has become one of the world's major economic powers with the greatest potential, and its overall living standards have reached that of a relatively well-off society. China has adopted the "Five-Year Plan" strategy for economic development, and altogether implemented nine Five-Year Plans from 1953 to 2000, laying a solid foundation for the country's economic development. The 10th Five-Year Plan (2001-2005) was remarkably successful in spurring China to enter the ranks of the world's strongest economies. Now the country is undertaking its 11th Five-Year Plan (2006-2010).

The Chinese government has strengthened and improved its macro-control, and China's economy has maintained its steady and rapid growth into the 21st century. The gross domestic product (GDP) for 2007 amounted to 24,953 billion yuan, 11.9% higher than the previous year.

Sketch Map Showing Regional Investment in Fixed Assets

Xinjiang

Northeastern Region

Beijing

Western Region

Eastern Region

Central Region

Tibe

Yunnan   Guangdong   Taiwan
Guangxi   Hong Kong
Macao

Hainan

South China Sea Is.

The Three Industrial Sectors

Primary Industry refers to agriculture, forestry, husbandry and fishery; Secondary Industry refers to mining, manufacturing, electric power, gas and fuel, water production and supply, and construction; and Tertiary Industry refers to service industries other than primary and secondary industries.

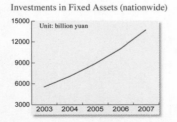

Investments in Fixed Assets (nationwide)

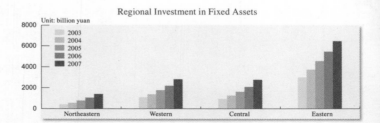

Regional Investment in Fixed Assets

Sketch Map Showing GDP and Employed Population in Different Regions

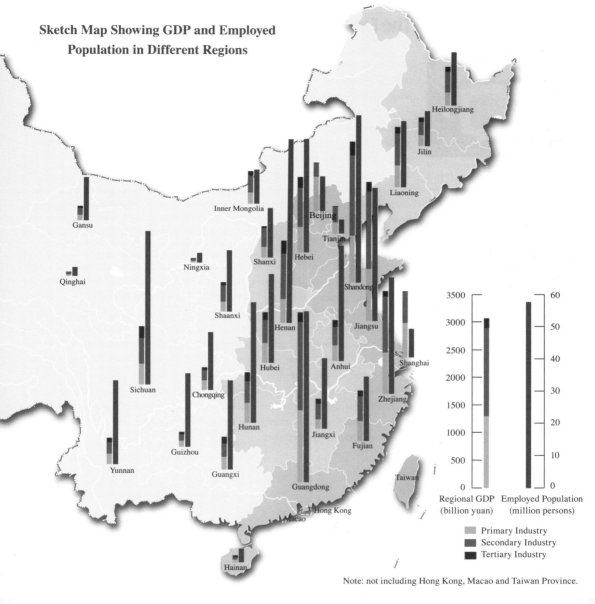

Gansu

Inner Mongolia

Beijing

Tianjin

Heilongjiang

Jilin

Liaoning

Ningxia

Shanxi

Hebei

Qinghai

Shaanxi

Shandong

Henan

Jiangsu

Hubei

Anhui

Shanghai

Sichuan

Chongqing

Zhejiang

Hunan

Jiangxi

Fujian

Guizhou

Yunnan

Guangxi

Guangdong

Taiwan

Hong Kong

Macao

Hainan

3500	60
3000	50
2500	40
2000	30
1500	20
1000	10
500	0
0	

Regional GDP   Employed Population
(billion yuan) (million persons)

Primary Industry
Secondary Industry
Tertiary Industry

Note: not including Hong Kong, Macao and Taiwan Province.

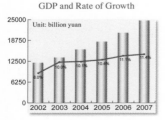

GDP and Rate of Growth

Unit: billion yuan

25000
18750
12500
6250
0

8.0% 10.0% 10.1% 10.4% 11.1% 11.4%

2002 2003 2004 2005 2006 2007

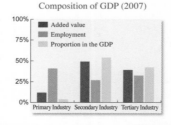

Composition of GDP (2007)

100%
75%
50%
25%
0%

Added value
Employment
Proportion in the GDP

Primary Industry   Secondary Industry   Tertiary Industry

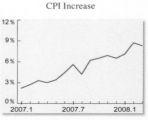

CPI Increase

12%
9%
6%
3%
0%

2007.1   2007.7   2008.1

The Economic System

On October 28, 2006, Industrial and Commercial Bank of China (ICBC) was listed in Shanghai and Hong Kong simultaneously.

In recent years, China's real estate industry has been developing fast. The picture shows a real estate sales office.

Economic restructuring is one of the most crucial elements in China's reform and opening-up policy. Economic reforms began in rural areas in 1978, and were extended to the cities in 1984. In 1992, the Chinese government clearly put forward the goal of economic system reform: to establish a socialist market economy.

The main principles of economic restructuring include encouraging economic development through various forms of ownership, while retaining the dominance of the public sector; creating a modern enterprise system to meet the requirements of the market economy; building a unified and open market system across China, linking domestic and international markets, and promoting optimized use of resources; transforming government economic management in order to establish a comprehensive macro-control system; encouraging some people in some regions to become rich first, to help all Chinese people become well off; and formulating a nationally appropriate social-security system for both urban and rural residents, so as to promote overall economic development and ensure social stability.

A socialist market economic system has now taken shape in China. The market is playing an increasingly important role in allocating resources, and the macro-control system is being refined; the public and non-public sectors of the economy, including individual-owned businesses and private companies, basically compose a commonly developed economic structure. According to plan, China is forecast to have in place a relatively complete socialist market economy by 2010, which will be relatively mature by 2020.

In 2008, the Chinese government has focused on four aspects of deepening economic system reform: promoting the reform of state-owned enterprises, and perfecting ownership structure; deepening reform of the finance and tax system, and accelerating construction of the public finance system; speeding up reform of the monetary system, while strengthening monetary supervision; expanding the depth and range of opening-up, while expanding the open economy.

The Scientific Outlook on Development

"The Scientific Outlook on Development" is a new slogan, frequently used by China's mass media in recent years. It is a concise expression of the governing concept of the new generation of the Central Authorities headed by Hu Jintao, as well as a key to the understanding of China's development and future trends.

"The Scientific Outlook on Development" takes development as its essence, putting people first as its core, with comprehensive, balanced and sustainable development as its basic requirement, and overall planning with due consideration for all concerned as its fundamental approach.

This means, we must pursue a scientific approach in development which should be comprehensive, balanced and sustainable. It requires us to promote not only economic development but also political, cultural, social and ecological development, to coordinate and give full consideration to all aspects, regions and links in our development, to conserve resources and protect the environment for better living and development space for future generations, to focus on improving people's livelihoods and promoting social justice, and to ensure that the fruits of development are shared among all China's 1.3 billion people.

Scientific Outlook on Development — A placard standing by the street

Opening up to the Outside World

In 1978, the Chinese government decided to implement a policy of gradual opening-up, while setting in motion economic restructuring. Since 1980, China has established five special economic zones in Shenzhen, Zhuhai and Shantou in Guangdong Province, Xiamen in Fujian Province, and Hainan Province; further opened up 14 coastal cities, a group of border area cities, and all provincial and regional capital cities; and set up 15 "bonded zones," 54 state economic and technological development zones, and 53 new- and high-technology industrial development zones in certain large and medium-sized cities. These areas have adopted different preferential policies, and serve as windows with a radiating influence on inland areas, for developing an export-oriented economy, generating foreign-exchange earnings through exports, and importing advanced technologies.

In 2000, China launched its "Develop the West" campaign. The western region includes Gansu, Guizhou, Ningxia, Qinghai, Shaanxi, Sichuan, Tibet, Xinjiang, Yunnan, Guangxi, Inner Mongolia, and Chongqing Municipality. It accounts for over 70% of China's total area and nearly 30% of its total population. Western China, bordered by more than 10 countries, is rich in land resources and mineral reserves. Hence it is believed that the west will become the next golden area for opening-up, after the development of eastern China's coastal areas. The Chinese government has instituted a series of preferential policies aiming at absorbing foreign investment in western areas, while drawing up a general plan for the development of western areas. In recent years, China's western areas have become a sweetener for foreign investors. By the end of 2007, over 3,000 foreign-invested enterprises have been founded in western areas, including the fields of logistics, IT, commerce, finance, security, trade, etc.

Foreign Exchange Reserve

Sketch Map Showing Opening-Up Cities and Areas

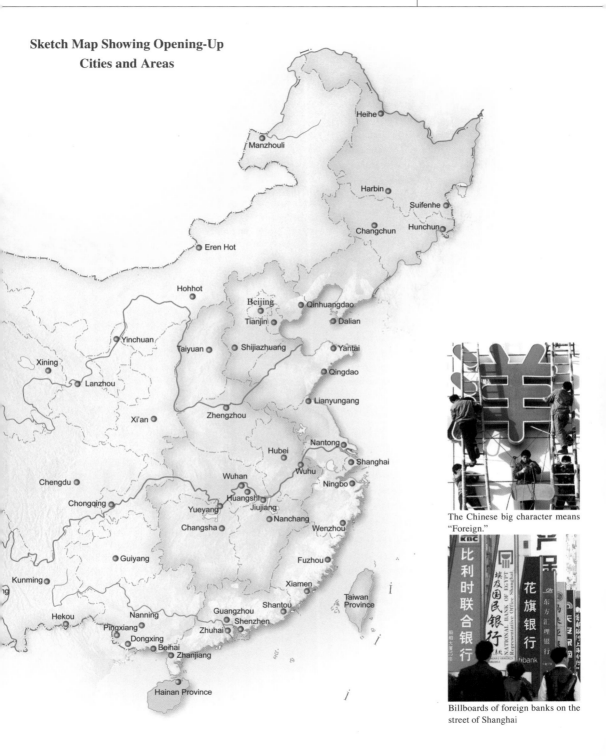

Heihe

Manzhouli

Harbin
Suifenhe
Changchun   Hunchun

Eren Hot

Hohhot

Beijing   Qinhuangdao
Tianjin   Dalian

Yinchuan   Taiyuan   Shijiazhuang   Yantai

Xining   Qingdao

Lanzhou   Lianyungang

Xi'an   Zhengzhou

Nantong
Hubei   Shanghai
Wuhu
Wuhan   Ningbo
Chengdu   Huangshi
Chongqing   Jiujiang
Yueyang   Nanchang
Changsha   Wenzhou

Guiyang   Fuzhou

Kunming   Xiamen

Shantou   Taiwan
Province
Hekou   Nanning   Guangzhou
Pingxiang   Shenzhen
Dongxing   Zhuhai
Beihai
Zhanjiang

Hainan Province

The Chinese big character means "Foreign."

Billboards of foreign banks on the street of Shanghai

Utilizing Foreign Capital

China utilizes foreign capital through various channels and forms in three major categories: 1) foreign loans, including loans from foreign governments, international financial institutions and foreign commercial banks, export credits, and issuance of bonds overseas; 2) direct foreign investment, including Chinese-foreign equity joint ventures, Chinese-foreign cooperative joint ventures, wholly foreign-owned enterprises and Chinese-foreign cooperative development projects; and 3) other foreign investment, including international leasing, compensation trade, processing and assembly, and issuance of stocks overseas. From 1979 to 2006, foreign capital utilized by China in real terms totaled US$ 882.7 billion, including US$ 691.9 billion of direct foreign investment. In 2007, foreign investment remained strong and foreign capital utilized in real terms for the year totaled US$ 78.3 billion, of which US$ 74.8 billion was direct foreign investment.

Since the 1980s, the NPC and the State Council have promulgated more than 500 foreign-related economic laws and regulations to provide legal and other guarantees for foreign investors in China. In accordance with the WTO rules and China's undertakings, the country has basically completed the rationalization and revision of foreign-related economic laws and regulations. A foreign-investment law system has been formed, its mainstay being the Law on Chinese-Foreign Equity Joint Ventures, the Law on Chinese-Foreign Cooperative Joint Ventures, the Law on Wholly Foreign-owned Enterprises, and the related rules for the implementation of these laws. By the end of 2007, foreign investors from nearly 200 countries and regions had established in China 591,000 foreign-funded enterprises. International financial groups and multinational companies see China as a top market; of the world's 500 top multinationals, over 450 have invested here. China has been hailed by investors and the financial world as a country with one of the best investment environments.

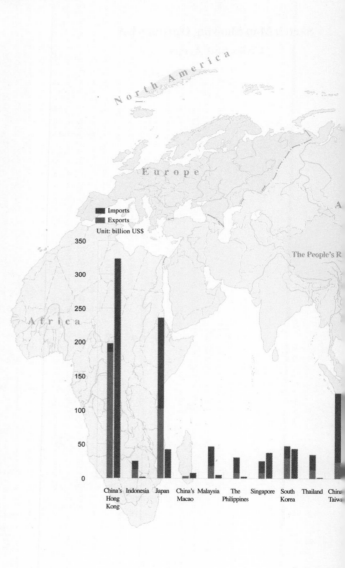

Sketch Map Showing Foreign Capital Utilization

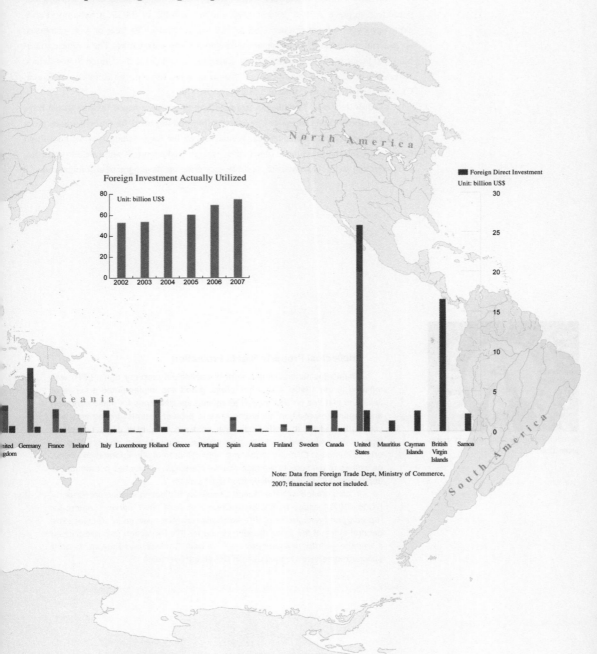

Foreign Investment Actually Utilized

Unit: billion US$

Foreign Direct Investment
Unit: billion US$

United Kingdom • Germany • France • Ireland • Italy • Luxembourg • Holland • Greece • Portugal • Spain • Austria • Finland • Sweden • Canada • United States • Mauritius • Cayman Islands • British Virgin Islands • Samoa

Note: Data from Foreign Trade Dept, Ministry of Commerce, 2007; financial sector not included.

Foreign Trade

In 2004, China's import-and-export trade volume ranked third in the world, compared to 27th place in 1978, 16th in 1990, and 8th in 2000. In 2007, China's import-and-export products volume reached US$ 2,173.8 billion with 23.5% year-on-year increases. At present, more than 230 countries and regions trade with China. The Chinese mainland's 10 major trading partners are: the European Union (EU), the United States, Japan, ASEAN, China's Hong Kong Special Administrative Region, the Republic of Korea, China's Taiwan Province, Russia, India and Australia.

On July 1, 2004, China began to implement the newly revised Foreign Trade Law. This law transformed the system of examination and approval for foreign trade into a registration system. It has made clear regulations on the import and export of goods and technology, international trade in services, foreign-trade controls and related protection of intellectual property rights, etc., so as to accelerate the development of foreign trade.

Symbol for intellectual property rights protection

Intellectual Property Rights Protection

China's institutionalized system of intellectual property rights (IPR) was initiated in the 1980s. China has promulgated and implemented a series of laws and statutes on IPR as well as related specifications for implementation and legal interpretation, including laws to protect patents, trademarks and copyright, statutes to protect computer software, integrated circuit layout design, audio and video products, new varieties of plants and intellectual property at customs, Olympic logos and rights to promulgate information online, as well as regulations to manage special markings. All this has contributed to improvements in China's IPR-related legal system.

In accordance with the "Action Outline for Protecting Intellectual Property (2006-2007)," issued by the State Council in April 2006, service centers for reporting and complaints of IPR violations have been set up in 50 cities. The general office of the State Working Group for IPR Protection also established a website — http://www.ipr.gov.cn — in both Chinese and English, to offer specialized services to the public in China and overseas.

Overseas Investment

According to statistics published by the Ministry of Commerce, China is transforming into a new country with extensive investments. By the end of 2007, China had direct overseas investments totaling US$ 93.7 billion (excluding financial investments); and the accumulated sales volume of its overseas contracting projects topped US$ 249.1 billion.

Direct overseas investment by China's enterprises is widening in scope, ranging from ordinary export trade, catering and simple processing, to sales networks, air logistics management, resource development, design and manufacturing, and research and development. China's investment regions have expanded to over 160 countries and regions. Transnational merger and acquisition has become the main channel for China's overseas investments. According to incomplete statistics, China's direct overseas investments through merger and acquisition amounted to US$ 17 billion in the first 11 months in 2007.

Some large enterprises and groups have become multinationals with relatively strong international competitiveness, through specialized, intensive and scaled transnational management, widening of resource configuration and strengthening of capability to participate in overseas economic cooperation. Such group companies include the China Petroleum and Chemical Company, State Grid Corporation of China and China National Petroleum Corporation.

The factory of China's Hisense Group in Johannesburg, South Africa

Reducing Tariffs

Since its entry into the WTO, China's overall level of customs duties on imports fell from 15.6% in 2000 to 9.9% in 2006. From January 1, 2007, China further reduced 44 import customs duties. While China's overall tariff levels have been reduced to 9.8%, the average tariff on agricultural products has decreased to 15.2%, and on industrial products, 8.95%.

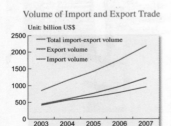

Volume of Import and Export Trade

Unit: billion US$
- Total import-export volume
- Export volume
- Import volume

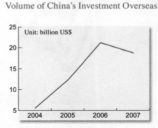

Volume of China's Investment Overseas

Unit: billion US$

Note: Financial sector not included.

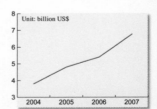

China's Labor Cooperation Overseas

Unit: billion US$

Diverse Economic Elements

A ship with a carrying capacity of 10,000 tons made by a privately-run enterprise in Wenling, Zhejiang Province was successfully launched.

Before 1978, state-owned and collective-owned enterprises represented 77.6% and 22.4%, respectively. The policy of reform and opening-up has given a wide scope to the common development of various economic sectors. By now, almost all state-owned enterprises have adopted a corporate governance system. Their impact in terms of control, influence and leadership in the overall national economy has been constantly increasing. In 2007, of the industrial added value created by all state-owned industrial enterprises and non-state industrial enterprises with annual sales revenue exceeding 5 million yuan, state-owned and state stockholding enterprises accounted for 39.2%, collective-owned enterprises 3.9%, with the rest taken up by other non-public enterprises, including enterprises with foreign, Hong Kong, Macao or Taiwan investments, and self-employed business and private enterprises. The result has been a dynamic juxtaposition of diverse economic elements.

In July 2007, of the Chinese enterprises ranking in the world's top 500, the 19 China's mainland enterprises were all state-owned. Of China's own top 500 enterprises, the majority were state-owned and state stockholding enterprises with business revenue accounting for 85.2% of the total, representing the main force of the Chinese economy. Non-state enterprises have become the main driving force for industrial sectors, the non-state economy accounting for 50% in 27 of the 40 industrial sectors, and more than 70% in some sectors.

Workshop of Alcatel Shanghai Bell

The 11th Five-Year Plan

Still underway, the "Outline of the 11th Five-Year Plan for National Economic and Social Development" lays out the blueprint for China's economic and social development during the period of the 11th Five-Year Plan (2006-2010) and sets the major indicators in this regard (see table below).

Major Indicators of Economic and Social Development During the 11th Five-Year Plan Period

Category	Indicators	2005	2010	Average Annual Growth Rate (%)	Note
Economic Growth	GDP (trillion yuan)	18.4	26.1	7.5	Anticipated
	Per-capita GDP (yuan)	14,103	19,270	6.6	Anticipated
Economic Structure	Ratio of Added Value of Service Industry (%)	40.3	43.3	[3]	Anticipated
	Employment Ratio of Service Industry (%)	31.3	35.3	[4]	Anticipated
	Expenditure on R&D Ratio of GDP (%)	1.3	2.0	[0.7]	Anticipated
	Urbanization Rate (%)	43	47	[4]	Anticipated
Population Resources and Environment	Total Population (10,000 people)	130,756	136,000	< 8‰	Obligatory
	Reduction of Consumption per Unit GDP (%)			[20]	Obligatory
	Reduction of Water Consumption per Unit Industrial Added Value (%)			[30]	Obligatory
	Efficient Utilization Coefficient of Agricultural Irrigation Water	0.45	0.50	[0.05]	Anticipated
	Comprehensive Utilization Ratio of Industrial Solid Waste (%)	55.8	60.0	[4.2]	Anticipated
	Total Cultivated Land (million ha)	122	120	-30	Obligatory
	Reduction of Total Major Pollutant Emission Volume (%)			[10]	Obligatory
	Forest Coverage (%)	18.2	20.0	[1.8]	Obligatory
Public Services and Quality of Life	Average Schooling Years of Citizens	8.5	9.0	[0.5]	Anticipated
	Population Covered by Basic Pension in Urban Areas (million people)	174	223	510	Obligatory
	Coverage of New Rural Cooperative Healthcare System (%)	23.5	> 80	> [56.5]	Obligatory
	Newly Increased Urban Employment in 5 Years (million people)			[45]	Anticipated
	Rural Labor Force Transferred in 5 Years (million people)			[45]	Anticipated
	Registered Urban Unemployment Rate (%)	4.2	5.0		Anticipated
	Per-capita Disposable Income of Urban Residents (yuan)	10,493	13,390	5.0	Anticipated
	Per-capita Net Income of Rural Residents (yuan)	3,255	4,150	5.0	Anticipated

Note: Figures of GDP and urban and rural residents' income are at 2005 prices; those in [ ] are cumulative figures of five years.

Agriculture

　　With only 7% of the world's cultivated land, China has successfully fed one fifth of the world's population. China's agriculture, therefore, takes a place of importance in the world.

　　Chinese agriculture has developed rapidly since reform in rural areas began in 1978. The major reforms were: the household responsibility system with remuneration linked to output, which restored to farmers the right to use land, arrange farm work, and dispose of their output; abolishing of state monopoly practices in purchase and marketing of agricultural products; removal of price restrictions on most agricultural and ancillary products; abolishing of many restrictive policies, allowing farmers to develop a diversified economy in rural areas and run township enterprises, so as to motivate greater enthusiasm for production. The reforms liberalized and developed rural productive forces, promoted the rapid growth of agriculture — particularly in grain production — and the continuous optimization of agricultural structure. The achievements have been remarkable. China now leads the world in output of grain, cotton, oil-bearing crops, fruit, meat, eggs, aquatic products, and vegetables.

　　With the continuous growth in the import and export trade of agricultural products, eight (including grains) out of the 15 categories of agricultural products, with trade volume accounting for 85 to 90 percent of the total trade volume of agricultural products, have shown a clear increase in net exports or a decrease in net imports. Aquatic products, vegetable and fruit have become competitive agricultural products of net export.

　　The goals of improving China's agricultural competitiveness, increasing the scale of agricultural industrialization

Output of Major Agricultural Produce

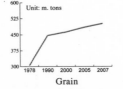

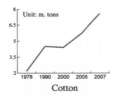

Sketch Map Showing Agricultural Output Value and Agricultural Population

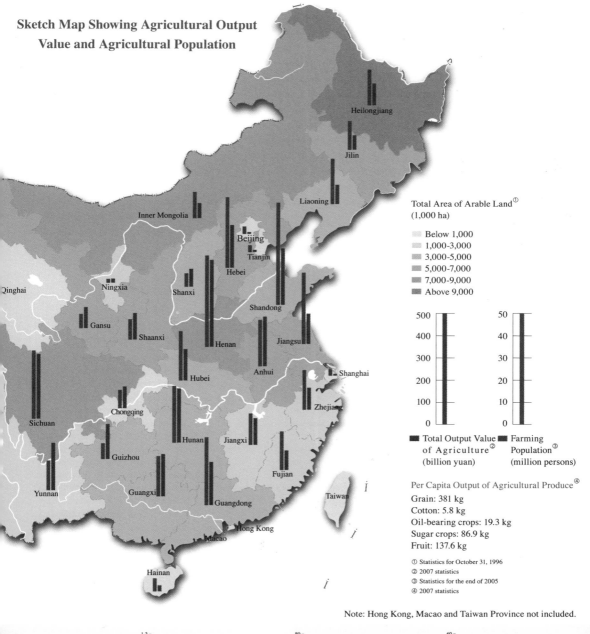

Total Area of Arable Land[1]
(1,000 ha)

- Below 1,000
- 1,000-3,000
- 3,000-5,000
- 5,000-7,000
- 7,000-9,000
- Above 9,000

■ Total Output Value of Agriculture[2]
(billion yuan)

■ Farming Population[3]
(million persons)

Per Capita Output of Agricultural Produce[4]
Grain: 381 kg
Cotton: 5.8 kg
Oil-bearing crops: 19.3 kg
Sugar crops: 86.9 kg
Fruit: 137.6 kg

[1] Statistics for October 31, 1996
[2] 2007 statistics
[3] Statistics for the end of 2005
[4] 2007 statistics

Note: Hong Kong, Macao and Taiwan Province not included.

Cured tobacco

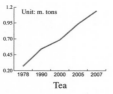

Tea

Meat

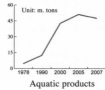

Aquatic products

Wheat harvesting in suburbs of Jinan, Shandong Province

Green house vegetable plantation

and promoting the all-round modernization of agriculture have been important issues for China's government in recent years. Now a pattern has been formed, spearheaded by some 600 key national enterprises, over 2,000 key provincial enterprises and multifarious agencies connecting farmers with the production base. Since 2003, the state has set up six types of demonstration projects, including industrialization of breeding and cultivation of top new varieties and fine strains, and of planting and breeding technology, etc., for industrialization of modern agro-technology, so as to boost the use of advanced technology for agricultural production, and to increase foreign earnings from export of farm products. Since 2006, the Ministry of Agriculture has accelerated the development of agricultural specialization and brands. Its goal is to encourage villages to develop leading agricultural products with distinct features, or famous agricultural brands. By so doing, can this facilitate economic construction in rural areas and the management of industrialized agriculture. So far, a large number of specialized export-oriented agricultural villages and townships have emerged in the eastern region, and many villages and townships specializing in cultivation and breeding have also begun to appear in the central and western regions.

Water-conserving Agriculture

Currently, Chinese agriculture uses 390 billion cubic meters of water a year, accounting for 70% of all the water used in China. Irrigation efficiency is only around 45%, so the water-conserving potential is enormous. The government water-conservation target is, by 2030, for irrigation efficiency to be a minimum of 55%, on the basis of no increase in the total amount of water consumed through agricultural use.

In the last 10 years, the government has paid a great deal of attention to demonstration work in agricultural water-conserving projects; established a range of national demonstration zones for agricultural water-conserving science and technology, high-tech demonstration parks for water-conserving agriculture, and water-conserving and high-yield demonstration zones; carried out follow-up support projects and technological reforms oriented towards water conservation in large-scale irrigation zones; and developed a variety of agricultural water-conserving development modes and technological systems for different types of zones. At the same time, the relevant governmental departments have extended water-conserving irrigation technologies, including channel seepage control, low-pressure pipeline water diversion, spray irrigation of large-scale farmland and drip irrigation under cotton film, in addition to such agricultural water-conserving technologies as straw mulch, plastic film, hydrogel, and drought-tolerant crops.

Promotion of Fine Breeds

The hybrid rice research achievements of Yuan Longping, a scientist internationally regarded as the "father of the hybrid rice," rewrote the history of rice-growing in China in the second half of the 20th century. At present, this super-class hybrid rice (12,000 kg per ha) is being popularized on a large scale. Yuan Longping's new goal is to produce super-class hybrid rice with a yield exceeding 13,500 kg per ha, before 2010. In addition, thanks to the key project of "Breeding New Varieties of Super-yielding Agricultural Products," 655 new varieties, including rapeseed, peanut, wheat and corn, have been examined and approved by the government. The planting rate of fine varieties of main crops has surpassed 95%.

In 2008, the state will implement the special industrialization project of high-tech biological breeding. The project is to encourage the selected breeding of new varieties of main crops, livestock, aquatic products and trees, and make greater achievements in the industrialization of biological breeding.

Township Enterprises

Township enterprises are farmer-initiated enterprises in rural areas. Township enterprises are involved in many sectors, e.g., industry, agricultural processing, transportation and communications, construction, commerce and catering. Township enterprises take full advantages of competitively priced goods and services across the whole country. Currently, there are 23 million township enterprises in China; two thirds of enterprises with annual income of over 10 million yuan have their own research organs; and a range of well-known enterprises with innovation capability and intellectual property rights have also appeared.

Fuhuang Group, Anhui Province, a township enterprise which has increased its sales income by 10,000 times in the past ten years

Agricultural Tax Exemption Policies

On January 1, 2006, the Chinese government decided to abolish all agricultural taxes.

Total Profits of Township Enterprises

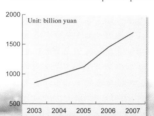

Yuan Longping, the "Father of Hybrid Rice" (member of the Chinese Academy of Engineering, and foreign associate of the US National Academy of Sciences)

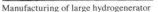

Manufacturing of large hydrogenerator

Assemble shop of FAW-VW Automobile Co., Ltd.

Industry

Since the beginning of reform and opening-up in 1979, China's industrial growth has maintained a high momentum. In 2007, industrial enterprises achieved industrial added value of 10,736.72 billion yuan, up 13.5% of that of the previous year. From January to November, industrial enterprises realized profits of 2,295.1 billion yuan, up 36.7% of that of the previous year. This revealed admirable simultaneous improvement in speed, quality and profits. Since 1996, China has led the world in output of steel, coal, cement, farm-use chemical fertilizers, and television sets.

Industrial Added Value and Rate of Growth

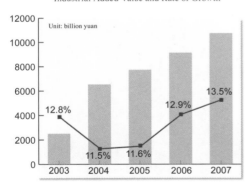

Output of Major Industrial Products

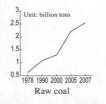

Raw coal

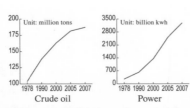

Crude oil

Power

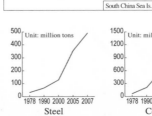

Steel

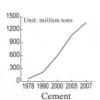

Cement

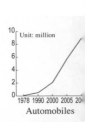

Automobiles

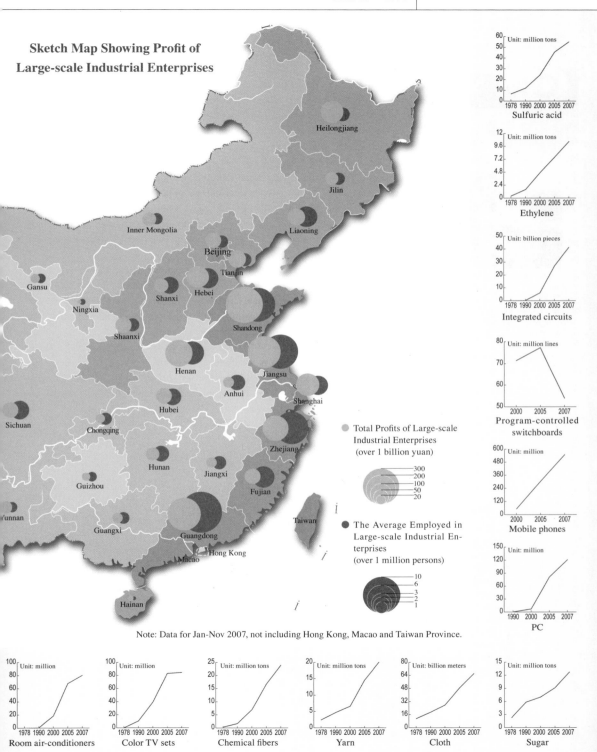

Sketch Map Showing Profit of Large-scale Industrial Enterprises

Total Profits of Large-scale Industrial Enterprises (over 1 billion yuan)

```
300
200
100
50
20
```

The Average Employed in Large-scale Industrial Enterprises (over 1 million persons)

```
10
6
3
2
1
```

Note: Data for Jan-Nov 2007, not including Hong Kong, Macao and Taiwan Province.

Sulfuric acid — Unit: million tons

Ethylene — Unit: million tons

Integrated circuits — Unit: billion pieces

Program-controlled switchboards — Unit: million lines

Mobile phones — Unit: million

PC — Unit: million

Room air-conditioners — Unit: million

Color TV sets — Unit: million

Chemical fibers — Unit: million tons

Yarn — Unit: million tons

Cloth — Unit: billion meters

Sugar — Unit: million tons

Energy Sector

The electric power industry is the fastest growing of all industrial sectors. At the end of 2007, the installed capacity of generators totaled 700 million kw, and the total generated electricity came to 3,277.7 billion kwh, ranking second in the world. Thermal power is the mainstay of electric power generation in China, while the installed capacity of hydro-power generators exceeds 145 million kw, ranking first in the world; the installed capacity of nuclear power generators also accounts for 8.85 million kw. China will build more nuclear generating facilities with 36 million kw capacity before 2020. Power-grid construction has entered its fastest-ever development, with 500-kv grids operating for inter-province and inter-region transmission and exchange. An international advanced control automation system, basically computerized, has been universally adopted, and has proven to be feasible. Now, China's power industry has entered a new era featuring large generating units, large power plants, large power grids, ultra-high voltage, and automation.

In February 2005, China's retail market of processed oil was opened in an all-round way. BP and other international oil giants entered Chinese market, establishing close contact with Chinese oil enterprises.

Since 1989, China has maintained its coal output at over one billion tons a year. China's coal industry now has the ability to design, construct, equip and administer 10-million-ton opencast coalmines and large and medium-sized mining areas. Coal washing and dressing technologies and capability have constantly been improved, along with coal liquefaction and underground gasification.

For 11 years running from 1997 to 2007, annual crude oil output exceeded 160 million tons, ranking China as fifth in the world. Oil industry development has accelerated the growth of local economies and related industries, such as machinery manufacturing, iron and steel industries, transport and communications. In 2007, China's natural gas output reached 69.3 billion cubic meters.

New Energy Resources

To relieve the shortage of energy supplies that fetters its economic growth, China is developing new energy resources according to different regional characteristics, such as wind, solar, geothermal, and tidal power. On January 1, 2006, the China Renewable Energy Law was launched, stipulating the responsibilities and duties of the government, enterprises and users in the development and exploration of renewable energy and the establishment of a series of policies and measures, including systems for overall objectives, special funding and preferential taxes. The Chinese government will progressively increase the consumption of high-quality, clean and renewable energy as a proportion of overall one-off energy consumption, from 7% in 2005 to 15% in 2020.

Astronautics

As the fifth country to develop and launch an independent manmade satellite and the third to master satellite recovery technology, China is in the world's front ranks in many important technological fields, including satellite recovery, carrying of multiple satellites on one rocket, rocket technology, and the launch, test and control of static-orbit satellites. Great achievements have been made in the manufacturing and application of remote-sensing satellites and communication satellites, and manned spacecraft. The successful launch of the Chang'e-1 lunar probe on October 24, 2007, and the first lunar image transmitted by Chang'e-1, published on November 26 by the China National Space Administration, symbolize that China has joined those select countries in the world capable of exploration in deep space. These achievements have been applied to serve all aspects of the national economy, such as meteorological satellite services.

The successful launch of the Chang'e-1 satellite, October 2007

Shenzhou V and Shenzhou VI, manned spacecraft developed independently by China, have been already successfully launched. Shenzhou VII is planned to be launched in October 2008 or so, and three astronauts will step out of the spaceship and complete spacewalks, rendezvous and docking in orbit. Up to the end of 2007, China successfully launched 110 independently developed satellites. China has developed 12 models of the Long March carrier rockets series, and is able to launch low earth orbit, geostationary orbit, and sun-synchronous orbit satellites and spaceships. The launch success rate is over 90%. China's exclusively home-developed Jiuquan, Xichang and Taiyuan satellite-launch centers are internationally recognized.

Yang Liwei, China's first astronaut

Long March 2-F carrier rocket, at the China International Industry Fair, Shanghai

Information Industry

By the end of 2007, China boasted 11.93 million domain names, of which 9 million were China-coded domain names, and 210 million internet users, ranking second in the world. A host of web-based services are thriving, for example, network education, online banking, e-commerce, internet advertising, news, video, and charged postal services, International Protocol (IP) telephone, SMS text-messaging, online recruitment, information services, and games. State and local governments have established data security and network credit systems for government administration, to satisfy the demand for inter-departmental, multi-application communications, resource sharing and application integration.

The information industry has become the leading mainstay of China's economy. In 2007, the added value of China's information industry, which is the world's third largest, stood at 1,363.8 billion yuan. Many Chinese products, including monitors, mobile phones and notebook computers, lead the world in terms of output. Statistics show that output value, sales and profits of electronic and telecom manufacturing have all outstripped those of traditional industries, making the greatest contribution to national economic growth.

Telephone

At the end of 2007, China had 912.74 million telephone subscribers, 365.45 million fixed lines and 547.29 million mobile phone subscribers, comprising the world's second-largest telephone network. Since China started up mobile telecommunication business in 1987, the mobile network now covers all urban and rural areas, with international roaming service with over 200 countries and regions all over the world.

A lama using a mobile phone

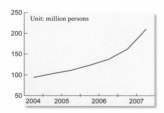
Number of Netizens
Unit: million persons

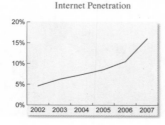
Internet Penetration

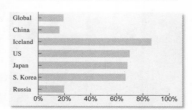
Internet Penetration in Selected Countries

Post and Telecommunications

A national postal network has taken shape, with Beijing and other major cities as centers, linking all cities and rural areas. As for the telecommunication network, a basic transmission network featuring large capacity and high speed is now in place. It covers the entire country, based on optical cables, supplemented by satellite and digital microwave systems. At the end of 2007, the total length of optical cables across China reached 5.74 million km. All provincial and autonomous regional capitals and over 90% of townships and cities are connected by an internet-mode optical cable network, which has become the main technology for transmitting information. Meanwhile, China has participated in the construction of a number of international land and sea-bed optical cables. Furthermore, China initiated the construction of the 27,000 km Asia-Europe optical cable, the world's longest land optical cable system, passing through 20 countries in its journey from Shanghai to Frankfurt in Germany. So far, China has established telecommunication business with more than 200 countries and regions in the world.

○ Telecommunication Capacity

Total length of optical cables:
  5.74 million km, including
  774,000 km of long-distance
  optical cables

Total number of broadband
internet access ports:
  85.392 million

International outlet bandwidth:
  368,927 M

Fixed-line penetration:
  27.8/ 100 persons

Home-phone penetration:
  21.1/ 100 persons

Mobile-phone penetration:
  41.6/ 100 persons

Precentage of administrative
villages with telephone service:
  99.5%

Express Mail Service

50.4 m. Netizens browsing the Internet using mobile phones account for 24.0% of the total.

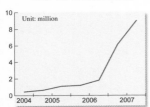

Total ".cn" Domain Names

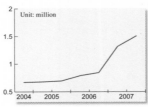

Number of Websites

Note: not including edu.cn data

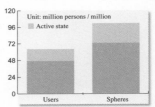

Blog Users and Blog Spheres

Communications and Transportation

Highways

Highways are China's key infrastructure construction. Beijing, Shanghai and other municipalities directly under the Central Government and all provincial capitals are being connected by highways, mainly expressways. Over 200 cities are connected by the network. By the end of 2007, the total length of highways had reached 3.584 million km, including 53,900 km of expressways, ranking China the second in the world. In 2007, a grid of five north-south and seven east-west arteries, totaling 35,000 km, was completed; 8,300 km of expressways have been built, and 423,000 km of rural highways have also been built or reconstructed.

The aim of the National Expressway Network Plan, approved by the State Council in early 2005, is an expressway system connecting all provincial capitals with Beijing and each other, linking major cities as well as important counties. The network will have a total length of about 85,000 km, including seven routes originating in Beijing — the Beijing-Shanghai, Beijing-Taibei, Beijing-Hong Kong-Macao, Beijing-Kunming, Beijing-Lhasa, Beijing-Urumuchi, and Beijing-Harbin expressways. By 2010, China will have built more than 24,000 km of expressways, and the network skeleton will have taken shape.

Sketch Map of Highway Network

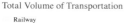

Total Volume of Transportation

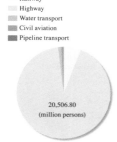

Volume of passenger turnover   Volume of freight turnover

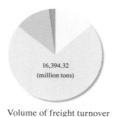

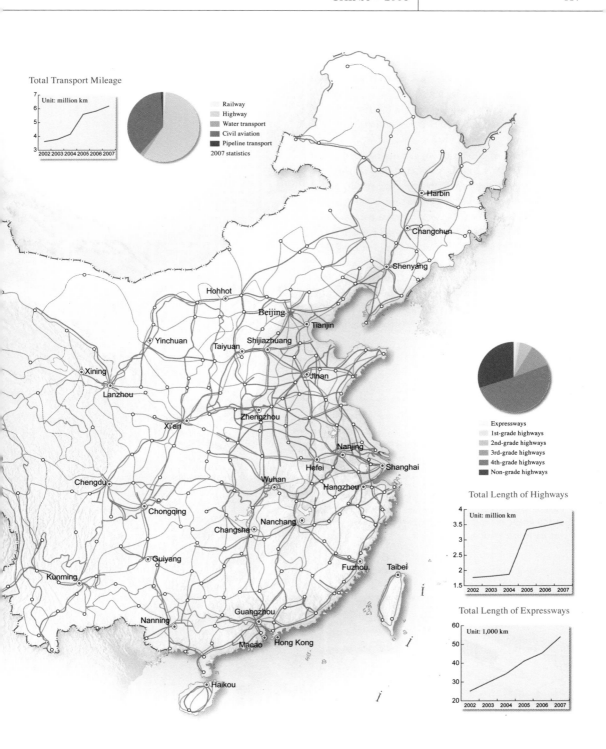

Total Transport Mileage

Unit: million km

7
6
5
4
3
2002 2003 2004 2005 2006 2007

Railway
Highway
Water transport
Civil aviation
Pipeline transport
2007 statistics

Expressways
1st-grade highways
2nd-grade highways
3rd-grade highways
4th-grade highways
Non-grade highways

Total Length of Highways

Unit: million km

4
3.5
3
2.5
2
1.5
2002   2003   2004   2005   2006   2007

Total Length of Expressways

Unit: 1,000 km

60
50
40
30
20
2002   2003   2004   2005   2006   2007

Railways

On a global basis, China's rail transport volume is one of the world's highest, carrying 25% of the world's total railway load, despite only having 6% of the world's operating railways. China also leads in terms of the growth rate of transport volume and in the efficient use of transport equipment.

At the end of 2007, railways in operation reached 78,000 km, including 24,400 km of electrified railways, the scale of China's electrified railway being second only to that of Russia and Germany. In 2007, China's newly built railways put into operation reached 678 km; dual tracks put into operation totaled 480 km; and electrified railways put into operation came to 938 km. According to the Mid- and Long-Term Railway Network Program approved by the State Council, China's railways in operation will reach 100,000 km by 2020.

The top speed of express trains has increased from 130 kmph to 200 kmph, with passenger trains capable of reaching a maximum speed of 250 kmph on certain sections of trunk railways.

Qinghai-Tibet Railway

On July 1, 2006, the Qinghai-Tibet Railway went into operation. It set a series of new records in world railway history: passing through a 960km-long section 4,000 meters above sea level; the highest plateau railway, 1,956 km long, with the highest spot of 5,072 meters; and passing through the permafrost section at 100 kmph, the top speed for railways through frozen earth in the world.

Sketch Map of Railway Network

"Train of Harmony," China's High-Speed bullet train

The Qinghai-Tibet Railway

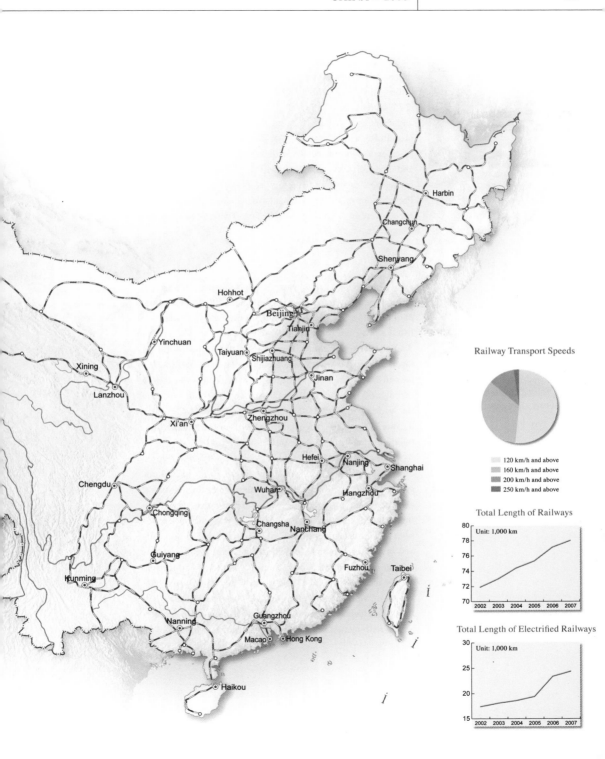

Railway Transport Speeds

120 km/h and above
160 km/h and above
200 km/h and above
250 km/h and above

Total Length of Railways

Unit: 1,000 km

Total Length of Electrified Railways

Unit: 1,000 km

Urban Light Rail

In a few years from now, the state will plan to construct urban rails of 500 to 600 km, with a total investment of 170 billion yuan. It is estimated that the length of light rail transit (LRT) across the country will reach close to 1,000 km by 2010, and about 2,000 km by 2020; by 2050, the total length of completed LRT will be around 4,500 km. At that time, these LRTs in cities will be integrated with subways, suburban railways and other rail systems, into a swift traffic urban track system, taking 50% to 80% of the total load of public traffic in cities. Presently, several LRT systems have also been completed and put into use in large cities like Beijing, Tianjin, Shanghai and Chongqing.

Maglev train in Shanghai

Ports

China has 13 ports, with freight volume exceeding 100 million tons a year. The ports of Shanghai, Shenzhen, Qingdao, Tianjin, Guangzhou, Xiamen, Ningbo and Dalian are listed among the world's top 50 container ports. The Port of Shanghai has maintained the first position in the world for three successive years, with freight volume of 560 million tons in 2007. The scale of China's merchant fleet has broken through 60 million deadweight tonnage, ranking fourth in the world. The tonnage of shipbuilding reached 14.52 million deadweight tonnage, accounting for 19% of the world's shipbuilding market and ranking third.

The construction of China's coastal ports has focused on transport systems for coal, containers, iron ore imports, grain, RORO operations between the mainland and islands, and deep-water access to the sea — in particular, strengthening container transport systems. The coal transport system has been further strengthened with the construction of coal loading and unloading wharves. In addition, wharves handling crude oil and iron ore imports have been reconstructed and expanded. By the end of 2007, China's coastal ports had over 3,800 berths, of which over 1,000 were 10,000-ton-class berths; their handling capacity achieved 111.79 million standard containers a year, ranking first in the world for the fifth year running.

Nansha Port, Guangzhou

Sketch Map of River and Sea Ports

Heilong River

Heihe ●

Songhua River

Harbin ●

Qinhuangdao ●

Beijing ★

Dalian ●

Tianjin ●

Yantai ●

Grand Canal

Qingdao ●

Yellow River

Jining ●   Rizhao ●

Lianyungang ●

Yangzhou ●   Nantong ●

Nanjing ●

Shanghai ●

Wuhu ●   Suzhou ●

Yangtze River   Wuhan ●   Hangzhou ●

Chongqing ●   Ningbo ●

Jiujiang ●

Yibin ●   Wenzhou ●

Fuzhou ●

Jilong ●

Quanzhou ●

Xiamen ●

Wuzhou ●

Guangzhou ●   Shantou ●

Pearl River   Shenzhen ●   Gaoxiong ●

Beihai ●   Hong Kong

Zhanjiang ●

Haikou ●

Dongfang ●

Sanya ●

Navigable rivers
Major coastal ports
Major river ports
Every 100 million tons of freight turnover
: not including Hong Kong, Macao and Taiwan Province.

Terminal 3 of Beijing Capital Airport

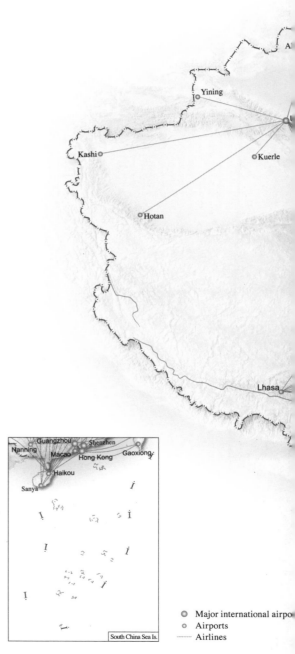

Civil Aviation

China has a total of 1,506 civil flight routes, 1,216 of them domestic routes reaching all large and medium-sized cities, and 290 international flights connecting the country with more than 91 cities overseas. China has signed agreements on air transport with 106 countries, including 51 countries with 93 airlines reaching 31 cities in China's mainland. At the end of 2007, China had 152 airports for civil flights. That year, the volume of passenger traffic reached 185.762 million persons and the volume of freight traffic totaled 4.019 million tons.

Although airline companies for civil flights are mainly state-run in China, more and more government backing is being given to private and jointly owned airlines involving both Chinese and foreign investment. At present, five private airline companies and six jointly owned Chinese-foreign airlines have gone into operation.

Total Civil Aviation Mileage

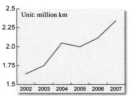

Total Aviation Passengers

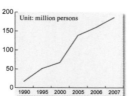

○ Major international airpo[rts]
○ Airports
----- Airlines

Sketch Map of Domestic Flight Routes

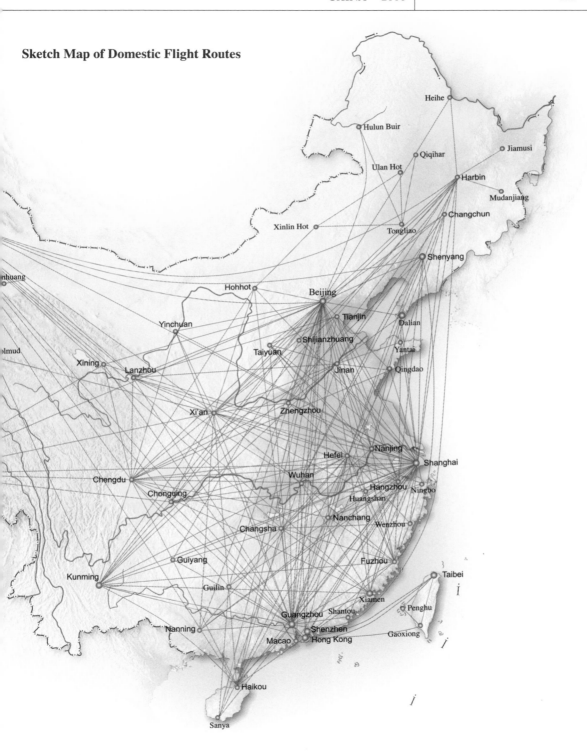

Stockholm
Amsterdam Copenhagen
London
Brussels Berlin Moscow
Paris Munich Frankfurt
Milan Vienna
To Sao Paulo Madrid Rome
Beirut
Teheran
Baghdad
Cairo
Riyadh Kuwait
Dubai
Khartoum
Djibouti
Addis Ababa
Irkutsk
Ulan Bator
Urumqi
Beijing
Pyongyar
Seoul Osaka
Pusan
Fukuoka Hiros
Shanghai
Karachi New Delhi Kunming Xiamen
Calcutta Guangzhou
Bombay Hanoi Hong Kong
Rangoon
Bangkok Manila
Kuala Lumpur
Singapore
Jakarta
Darwin
Melb

Sketch Map of Major International
Flight Routes

Anchorage

Vancouver

Seattle

Chicago

New York

Washington D.C.

San Francisco

Los Angeles

Lima

Rio de Janeiro

Sao Paulo

via Madrid to Beijing

San Diego

Buenos Aires

resby

Suva

Papeete

Oakland

Finance and Insurance

Financial System

China has basically formed a financial system under the regulation, control and supervision of the central bank, with state banks as the mainstay, featuring the separation of policy-related banks and commercial banks, and the cooperation of various financial institutions with mutually complementary functions. The People's Bank of China no longer handles credit and savings business, but exercises a central bank's functions and powers by conducting macro-control and supervision over the nation's banking system. The Industrial and Commercial Bank of China, the Bank of China, the Agricultural Bank of China and the Construction Bank of China are state-owned commercial banks; while the Agricultural Development Bank of China, the National Development Bank and the China Import and Export Bank are three policy-related banks. The commercial banks wholly owned by the state have subsequently set up or reorganized over 120 shareholding medium and small-sized commercial banks, and further standardized and developed securities and insurance financial institutions. In 2006, the China Postal Savings Bank was established, focusing on developing retail and intermediary businesses, to offer basic financial services for residents in urban and extensive rural areas, and set up complementary networking with other commercial banks.

April 2003 saw the formal establishment of the China Banking Regulatory Commission (CBRC). Since then, a financial regulatory system has been formed in which the CBRC, the China Securities Regulatory Commission (CSRC) and China Insurance Regulatory Commission (CIRC) work in coordination, each body having its own clearly defined responsibilities. At the end of 2007, the balance of domestic and foreign currency savings deposits stood at 40,105.1 billion yuan, and the balance of domestic and foreign currency loans came to 27,774.7 billion yuan.

The People's Bank of China — China's reserve bank

Currency and Exchange Rates

The Renminbi (RMB), China's legal currency, is issued and controlled solely by the People's Bank of China. RMB exchange rates are decided by the People's Bank of China and issued by the State Administration of Foreign Exchange, the latter exercising the functions and powers of exchange control.

Through the reform of the foreign-exchange system, China has subsequently synchronized the official foreign-exchange rate with the adjusted foreign-exchange rate of the RMB, adopted the bank exchange settlement system, set up a unified inter-bank foreign-exchange market, and included the foreign-exchange business of foreign-invested enterprises in the bank's exchange settlement system. On December 1, 1996, China formally accepted Article 8 of the Agreement on International Currencies and Funds, and realized RMB convertibility under current accounts ahead of schedule. Meanwhile, China has been active in promoting bilateral currency exchange between ASEAN and China, Japan and the Republic of Korea (10+3). At the end of 2007, China's foreign-exchange reserves stood at US$ 1,528.2 billion, and China's share in the International Monetary Fund had risen from eighth to sixth place. The variety of financial business has grown steadily, and China has opened an array of new types of business, to become integrated into the various aspects of modern international finance, including consumer credit, securities investment funds and insurance-linked investments.

Lu Jiazui Finance and Trade Zone, Pudong, Shanghai, with banks standing in great numbers

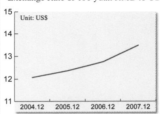

Exchange Rate of 100 yuan RMB to US$

China's Commercial Banks Overseas

In 1980, China resumed membership in the World Bank, and returned to the International Monetary Fund. In 1984, China started business contacts with the Bank for International Settlements; in 1985, China formally became a member of the African Development Bank, and in 1986, of the Asian Development Bank. By the end of June 2007, all China's main commercial banks have set up over 110 branches in nearly 30 countries and regions, and developed international credit business.

Foreign Banks in China

By the end of 2007, 26 foreign investment banks had been established in China, with 125 branches and 160 sub-branches; foreign banks have set up 117 branches and 9 sub-branches. The CBRC has approved the conversion of the branches of 21 foreign investment banks in China into the banks with legal person status, of which 17 completed such conversion and commenced operations. To date, six transformed foreign investment banks have been allowed to handle RMB transactions and five transformed foreign investment banks have been allowed to handle bankcard business.

Securities

In 1990 and 1991, China set up securities exchanges in Shanghai and Shenzhen. Over the past decade, the Chinese stock market has matured, completing a journey that took many countries a hundred years or more to navigate. The Chinese stock market has promoted the reform of state-owned enterprises and changes to their systems, and enabled a stable transition between the two systems. As for ordinary citizens, the stock market has joined bank deposits to become one of the most important channels for investment.

Chinese stockholders

Today, a network system for securities exchange and account settlement has been formed, with the Shanghai and Shenzhen exchanges as the powerhouse, radiating to all parts of the country. The modes of technology have reached advanced world standards, with realization of scriptless trading. According to 2007 statistics, there were 1,550 listed companies, with a total market value of 32,714.1 billion yuan. China issued 283 kinds of "A shares," and seven rights issues, collecting a total of 772.8 billion yuan; and 14 kinds of "H shares," collecting a total of 70.4 billion yuan.

One of the first established insurance companies in China

Insurance

The insurance industry in China recovered in 1980, after 20 years of standstill. In 1981, the People's Insurance Company of China was transformed from a government department into a specialized company, with branches or sub-branches in every part of the country. The year 1988 saw the founding of the Ping An Insurance (Group) Company of China, and the Pacific Insurance Company, both operating mainly in the coastal areas; and 2003 saw the establishment of the PICC Property and Casualty Company Limited and China Life Insurance Company Limited. The promulgation of the Insurance Law in 1995 and the establishment of the China Insurance Regulatory Commission in 1998 have provided the legal basis and specific rules for the smooth operation of the insurance market. In 2007, there were 110 insurance companies nationwide, with premium revenues totaling 703.6 billion yuan, and compensation and expenditure totaling 226.5 billion yuan.

China's insurance industry has actively explored the international market, setting up 43 operational offices and 9 representative offices in Southeast Asia, Europe and North America.

Stock Value on Stock Market

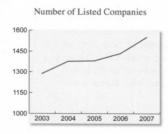

Number of Listed Companies

Number of Stockholders and Fund Purchasers

① Up to September 4, 2007
② Up to account-opening of A-shares at the end of June 2007

Tourism

Tourist Market

Today, China has one of the largest domestic tourism markets in the world, with the highest rate of growth. In 2007, the number of incoming tourists reached 131.87 million person-times, of which foreigners numbered 26.11 million, making China the fourth-largest tourist-intake country in the world; foreign-exchange revenue from tourism rose to US$ 41.9 billion, ranking sixth in the world; domestic tourists numbered 1.61 billion person-times, with domestic tourism revenue amounting to 777.1 billion yuan.

China's outbound tourism is the fastest growing of any emerging tourist source in the world, and China is Asia's leading source country for outbound tourism. So far, China has approved 134 countries and regions as tourist destinations for Chinese citizens traveling at their own expense; of these, 91, including the United States and more than 30 European countries, can be easily reached. The average consumer expenditure of Chinese citizens traveling abroad has become one of the highest in the world. According to the statistics of China Travel Monitor, under IPK International, the daily expenses of Chinese tourists during a long holiday top the world average.

Badaling Great Wall, Beijing

Number of Foreign Tourists

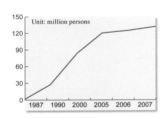

Foreign Currency Income from International Tourism

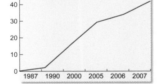

Number of Outbound Tourists

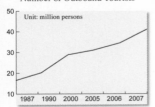

Per Capita Consumption of Outbound Tourists

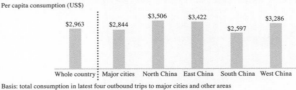

Per capita consumption (US$)

	Whole country	Major cities	North China	East China	South China	West China
Per capita consumption	$2,963	$2,844	$3,506	$3,422	$2,597	$3,286
Number of sample (weighted)	6030	2256	797	843	1387	747

Basis: total consumption in latest four outbound trips to major cities and other areas

Conversion formula: US$1=7.02 RMB (according to exchange rate on April 1, 2008); total consumption includes costs in preparation and on the trip, with average spending on shopping as US$800.

Source: "Nilson Report on Chinese Citizens' Outbound Tourism."

Chinese tourists arriving in Cheju Island, South Korea by the Royal Caribbean international "Rhapsody of the Seas"

The World Tourism Organization predicts that, by 2020 China will become the world's top tourist destination; and it will rank fourth in terms of outbound tourist numbers, with 100 million Chinese nationals traveling abroad every year. In November 2007, Chinese was approved as an official language by the United Nations World Tourism Organization (UNWTO), at the 17th session of the General Assembly.

Tourist Services

The rapid development of China's transport infrastructure has provided safe and convenient transportation for overseas and domestic tourists. Throughout China, great numbers of hotels have been constructed, renovated or expanded, to satisfy all levels of tourist requirements, and there are now more than 10,000 star-rated hotels. All large or medium-sized cities and scenic spots have hotels with full facilities and services for both domestic and international visitors.

China now has some 1,700 international travel agencies, with over 300 in Beijing, Shanghai, Tianjin and Chongqing. On June 12, 2003, the China National Tourism Administration (CNTA) and the Ministry of Commerce jointly put forward the "Interim Regulations on the Establishment of Foreign-controlled or Foreign-invested Travel Agencies." The first foreign-invested travel company to enter China's tourism market was JALPAK International China Co. Ltd. The first overseas-controlled joint venture in China's tourism industry was TUI China Travel Company, with its holding party being the largest European travel group TUI, and Martin Buese China Ltd., its Chinese partner being China Travel Service (CTS), which has a network of over 300 local offices.

Tourism Resources

China abounds in natural landscapes and places of cultural interest. The country has altogether 6 natural sites, 25 cultural sites and 4 mixed sites included in the World Heritage List; and 110 famous cultural cities, most of which are over 1,000 years old. China is made up of 56 different ethnic groups, with diverse cultures and customs. In Yunnan, Guizhou, Sichuan, Guangxi, Hunan, Hubei, Gansu, Ningxia, Tibet, Inner Mongolia and Xinjiang, with large minority communities, it is possible to see a great variety of folk cultures and customs.

Scenery of Lijiang River, Guilin, Guangxi

Major Tourism Routes

● Essential China Tour

Beijing, Shaanxi, Shanghai and Guangdong.

● China Health and Fitness Tour

Shanghai, Jiangsu, Hebei and Shaanxi, experiencing traditional Chinese medicine's acupuncture and massage, and learning *taijiquan*, or Chinese shadow-boxing, *taijijian* sword and fitness *qigong*.

● Great Wall Tour

From Beijing, Hebei and Ningxia to Gansu, visiting the better-preserved sections of the Great Wall.

● Religious Culture Tour

Mainly visiting renowned temples or monasteries, e.g., in Beijing, Shanxi, Anhui, Zhejiang, Sichuan, Hubei, Qinghai, and Tibet.

● Sea or Lake Holiday Tour

12 national tourist retreat areas, including Sanya in Hainan, Qingdao in Shandong Province, Dalian in Liaoning, Beihai in Guangxi, Putian and Wuyi Mountain in Fujian, and Kunming's Dianchi Lake.

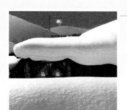

● Ice and Snow Tour

Liaoning, Heilongjiang and Jilin, to appreciate ice formations, ice lanterns and sculptures, as well as folk customs, and for skiing.

● Silk Road Tour

Urumqi, Xining, Yinchuan, Lanzhou and Xi'an, along the ancient Silk Road route.

● Central China Folk Customs Tour

Shanxi, Henan, Shandong and Beijing, highlights of folk villages and scenic sites.

Southwest China Folk Customs Tour

Yunnan, Guizhou, Guangxi and Sichuan, highlighting minority folk customs, villages and scenic sites.

Three Gorges Tour

Along the Yangtze River to Chongqing, Sichuan, Hunan and Hubei, visiting renowned natural and cultural sites in the Three Gorges region.

South China Riverside Village Tour

Hangzhou, Jiaxing and Shaoxing in Zhejiang Province, and Nanjing, Yangzhou, Wuxi and Suzhou in Jiangsu Province, experiencing local conditions and customs.

Folk Customs Tour

Along the Yellow River to Qinghai, Gansu, Ningxia, Shanxi, Inner Mongolia, Henan and Shandong, visiting renowned natural and cultural sites.

Landscape Tour

Fujian, Guangxi, Anhui, Guizhou, Hunan, Jilin and Sichuan, visiting renowned natural and cultural sites.

Environmental Protection

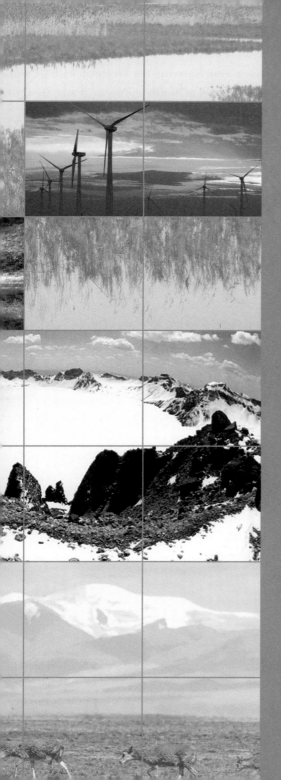

Laws and Systems for Environmental Protection

The Constitution of China clearly specifies: "The state protects and improves the environment in which people live and the ecological environment. It prevents and controls pollution and other public hazards." Environmental protection has been a basic national policy since the 1980s. The first Environmental Protection Law was issued in 1989. So far, the NPC and the State Council have promulgated nine laws for environmental protection, 15 laws for management of natural resources and 50 regulations on environmental protection. Related departments under the State Council have issued over 100 national environmental protection regulations; and local people's congresses and governments have also promulgated more than 1,000 regulations to refine the environmental protection legal system. Furthermore, a central and local system of environmental protection standards also has been set up across the whole country. The State Environmental Protection Administration has now been upgraded as the Ministry of Environmental Protection.

The management system for environmental protection implemented in China includes: governments at all levels taking charge of local environmental quality, administrative departments of environmental protection exercising unified supervision and related departments implementing supervision and administration according to the law. The state has instituted a system of inter-ministerial joint conferences for environmental protection, and established representative offices for regional environmental protection supervision to enhance coordination and cooperation between departments and regions.

Sketch Map Showing the Western, Middle and Eastern Routes of South-to-North Water Diverting

→ Water flow direction in south-to-north water diverting projects

| Unit: per ton standard coal/ 10,000 yuan (not including HK, Macao and Taiwan Province) | Whole country | Beijing | Tianjin | Hebei | Shanxi | Inner Mongolia | Liaoning | Jilin | Heilongjiang | Shanghai | Jiangsu | Zhejiang | Anhui | Fujian |

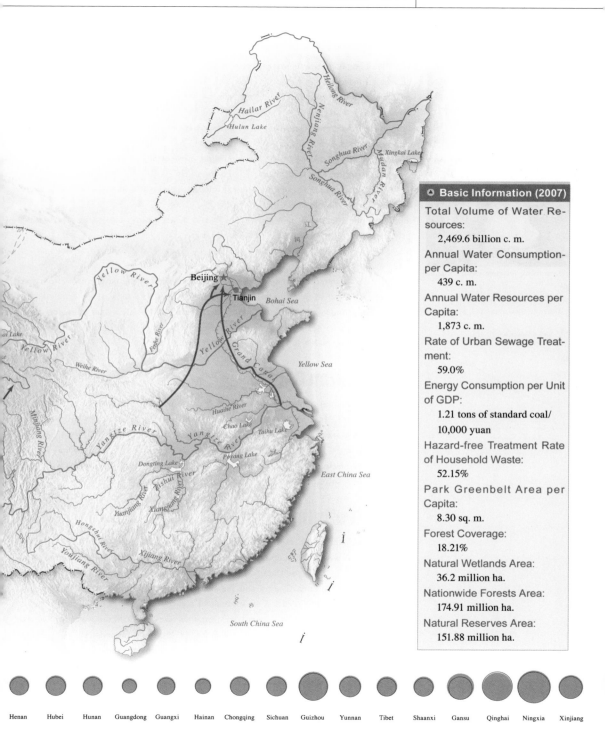

Basic Information (2007)

Total Volume of Water Resources:
2,469.6 billion c. m.

Annual Water Consumption per Capita:
439 c. m.

Annual Water Resources per Capita:
1,873 c. m.

Rate of Urban Sewage Treatment:
59.0%

Energy Consumption per Unit of GDP:
1.21 tons of standard coal/ 10,000 yuan

Hazard-free Treatment Rate of Household Waste:
52.15%

Park Greenbelt Area per Capita:
8.30 sq. m.

Forest Coverage:
18.21%

Natural Wetlands Area:
36.2 million ha.

Nationwide Forests Area:
174.91 million ha.

Natural Reserves Area:
151.88 million ha.

Henan   Hubei   Hunan   Guangdong   Guangxi   Hainan   Chongqing   Sichuan   Guizhou   Yunnan   Tibet   Shaanxi   Gansu   Qinghai   Ningxia   Xinjiang

Changpuhe Park, Beijing

Citizens using reusable cloth shopping bags

Investment in Environmental Management

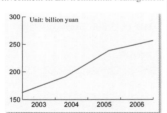

New Changes in Environmental Protection

Traditional environmental protection methods are being transformed in the process of gradual perfecting of the environmental protection legal system. The earlier end-of-pipe treatment system and remedial management modes are being transformed into over-all monitoring and control. In 1998, Regulations for the Administration of Environmental Protection Concerning Construction Projects, promulgated by the Chinese government, clearly details the environment-impact-assessment system, and the simultaneous design-ing, construction and use of the environmental-protection facilities together with the construction of the relevant project. The Environment Impact Assessment Law, issued in 2003, expanded the system of environment impact assessment from construction projects into all sorts of development and construction programs, and stipulates that feasibility-study meetings, hearings and other forms should be introduced to discuss construction projects or programs with possible adverse impacts.

The main entities for environmental protection in China present a diversified struc-ture. Widespread participation from enterprises, science and technology institutions and NGOs has advanced the shaping of a phase that is being led by the government, promoted by enterprises, joined by the public, supported by science and technology, regulated by laws and adjusted by the market. Environmental-protection NGOs and volunteers have played significant roles in environmental protection. Currently, the number of environ-mental-protection NGOs in China totals about 1,000.

Air Pollution Control

Environmental quality has seen great improvement, thanks to years of sustained pollution control. In 2007, the total volume of sulfur-dioxide emissions decreased by 4.66%. In November 2007, the State Council issued the National 11th Five-Year Plan for Environmental Protection which stipulates the need to actively build projects for the enhancement of environmental supervision capability and control greenhouse gas emis-sions. By 2010, sulfur-dioxide emissions will be basically brought under control.

Water Pollution Control

The National 11th Five-Year Plan for Environmental Protection prioritizes the reha-bilitation of rivers and lakes and guaranteeing of safety of drinking water for urban and rural residents. In 2007, the state invested thousands of millions of yuan to fully launch the Water Body Pollution Control and Treatment Program, focusing on the three major fields of drinking-water security, environmental control of river basins and urban water pollution treatment. The government will strengthen work on drinking-water security in the countryside, striving to solve this problem for 300 million rural people.

Since 2003, the State Environmental Protection Administration (now Ministry of Environmental Protection) has published annual updates on pollution control in national key river basins and sea areas. Owing to years of effective control of water pollution, there has been clear improvement to the water environment in the seriously polluted

Energy Conservation and Pollution Emission Reduction

Between 2006 and 2010, China plans to reduce energy consumption per unit of GDP by 20%, and total volume of major pollution emissions by 10%. These goals have legal binding force. Thus, 2007 saw the country's swift adjustments of its industrial structure and control of overly rapid growth in industries with high consumption and high pollution emissions; the same year also witnessed the quick implementation of ten major energy-conservation projects and the launching of energy-saving activities among a thousand enterprises.

The year 2007 saw a "national campaign of energy conservation and pollution emissions reduction," calling on all people to participate in such efforts. In this campaign, government offices took the lead in carrying out the principle of "green work" to guide people in fulfilling energy-conservation obligations, by starting from small things, such as reducing car or paper use to the minimum, and saving electricity as much as possible.

Taihu Lake, and the Yellow River has not run dry for six consecutive years. To ensure a safe water environment in the Three Gorges Reservoir Area, the government has planned to invest about 40 billion yuan between 2001 and 2010 to control water pollution in the reservoir area itself and the upper Yangtze.

Wind power installations in Xinjiang

Control of Desertification

The area of desertification in China, which is 4.38 million sq km or about 45% of the country's land territory, far exceeds its total farmland area. Years of hard work are beginning to produce results. Between November 2003 and April 2005, the State Forestry Administration carried out the third nationwide monitoring of land degradation and sand encroachment, which showed that the areas affected by both had been lessened for the first time since the founding of PRC in 1949, and that the overall desertification trend was beginning to be stemmed.

The State Forestry Administration has implemented a nationwide sand-control program, aiming to achieve basic control of desertification by 2010.

Solar energy utilization in China

China has spared no efforts in treating sewage; the picture shows a newly built sewage treatment plant in Zhejiang.

Protection of Forest Resources

Local people in Minqin, Gansu Province, compressing straw and planting sacsaoul trees to combat desertification

Forest Coverage Rate

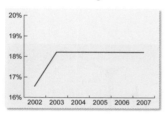

Since the 1950s, China has made amazing achievements in cultivated forests. Currently, China has 57.45 million ha of reserved planted forests, ranking the first in the world, with a forest coverage rate of 18.21%. While many countries have seen a decline in forest resources, China has increased both the area and reserves of its forests and was listed by the United Nations Environment Program as one of the 15 countries preserving the greatest area of forests. An effective measure in forest protection is the natural forest conservation program started in 1998, which stipulated a nationwide end to the felling of trees in natural forests. In many areas, lumbermen of the past have now become rangers.

Nature Reserves

China's first nature reserve, established in 1956, was the Dinghu Mountain Nature Reserve in Zhaoqing, Guangdong Province. By the end of 2007, there were 2,531 nature reserves of various kinds established throughout the country, accounting for 15% of the country's territory, of which 303 are state-level nature reserves. Protected through these nature reserves are 88% of China's land eco-system, 87% of its wildlife population, 65% of its higher plant communities, nearly 20% of its natural forests, 50% of its marshlands and wetlands, the main habitats of more than 300 precious and endangered wild animal species, and major distribution areas for over 130 precious tree varieties.

Established in August 2000, the Sanjiangyuan Nature Reserve has the greatest concentration of bio-diversity of all of China's nature reserves. Covering an area of 31.6 million ha and with an average elevation of 4,000 m, it is also the largest and highest nature reserve. It is located in the central Qinghai-Tibet Plateau, at the source of the Yangtze, Yellow and Lancang rivers. State-level investment of 220 million yuan has been committed to the Sanjiangyuan protection project, which started in 2003. Guangdong Province has 294 nature reserves, the largest number in China, covering a combined area of 3.44 million ha. Wolong and Jiuzhaigou in Sichuan, Changbaishan Mountain in Jilin, Dinghushan Mountain in Guangdong and Baishui River in Gansu are among the 27 nature reserves that have been designated by UNESCO as "World Biosphere Reserves."

Protecting Endangered Animals and Plants

China has rich biodiversity, boasting the world's largest number of bird species and gymnosperm varieties. But China's biodiversity is faced with a critical situation: 15% to 20% of higher plant varieties are endangered, threatening the existence of 40,000 species of organisms associated with them.

Shennongjia Nature Reserve

As one of the earliest signatory countries to the Convention on Biological Diversity, China has been active in international affairs concerning the Convention and vocal on important issues related to biodiversity. China is also one of the few countries to complete the Convention's action plans. The China Action Plan for Biodiversity Conservation, implemented in 1994, has provided rules and regulations for many eco-environmental protection activities. According to the Law on the Protection of Wildlife, any criminal act damaging wildlife resources is subject to punishment.

The concerned government departments have focused on effective protection of biological resources, establishing over 400 centers for the raising of wild plant varieties or genetic protection, and artificially breeding thousands of wild plants. To help save endangered wildlife, 250 wildlife breeding centers have been established throughout the country, and special projects have been conducted to protect seven species, including the giant panda and crested ibis.

Yancheng Biosphere Reserve, Jiangsu

Wetland Protection

China has 65.94 million ha of wetlands, 36.20 million ha of which are natural wetlands, ranking first in Asia and fourth in the world. China's wetlands fall into 31 different types and nine categories. China's range of wetland types is among the widest in the world. Since joining the Ramsar Convention on Wetlands in 1992, the government has established 535 natural wetland reserves, thus bringing 40% of natural wetlands and 33 key animals within the nature reserves under effective state protection. Many nature reserves are low-lying beaches by seas, lakes and rivers and forest-margin wetlands; of these, 30, with a total area of 3.46 million ha, have been classified as "Wetlands of International Significance."

Nature Reserves

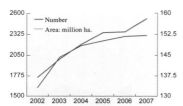

Number	
Area: million ha.	

Changbai Mountain

Shennongjia

Jiuzhaigou

Wuyi Mountain

Yellow River Delta

West Ujimqin Grassland

East Dongting Lake

Hoh Xil

Mount Cangshan and Lake
Erhai

Manasarovar Wetlands in
Tibet

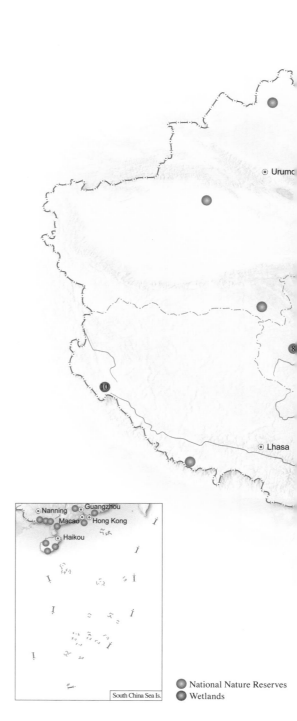

National Nature Reserves
Wetlands

Sketch Map Showing Distribution of Nature
Reserves and Wetlands

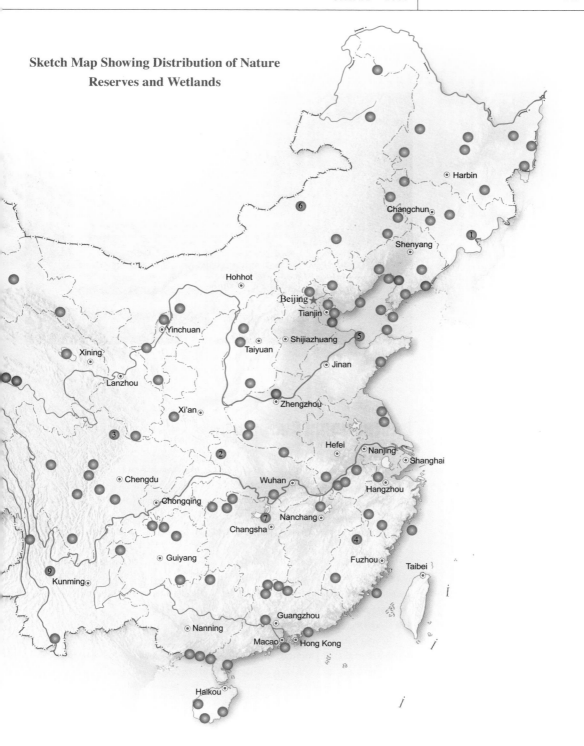

In 2007, the International Conference on Sustainable Sanitation was held in Beijing.

International Cooperation

China actively supports global environmental efforts and has played a constructive role in international environmental affairs. To date, China has participated in over 50 international conventions concerning environmental protection and played an active role in performing its obligations. The Chinese government has promulgated more than 100 policies and measures concerning the protection of the ozonosphere and achieved the gradual reduction goals stipulated in the Montreal Protocol on Substances that Deplete the Ozone Layer.

The China Council for Cooperation on Environment and Development was created by China, the first of its kind in the world. It consists of some 40 experts and serves as a senior consultancy for the government. Since its establishment more than a decade ago, it has made many constructive proposals to the Chinese government and is regarded overseas as a model for international environmental cooperation.

China actively participates in and promotes regional cooperation on the environmental protection, forming an initial cooperation framework with nearby countries. Positive progress has been made at various conferences, including the Tripartite China-

Japan-Korea Environment Ministers Meeting; the China-Europe Ministerial Dialogue on Environmental Policies; the ASEAN-China-Japan-Korea Environment Ministers Meeting; the Central Asia Environmental Cooperation Meeting; the Asia-Europe Ministers Meeting; the China-Arab Countries Working Conference; and in environmental cooperation mechanisms under the framework of the Shanghai Cooperation Organization.

China has carried out effective and successful cooperation, while maintaining good cooperative relations with the United Nations Environment Program (UNEP), the United Nations Development Program (UNDP), the Global Environment Facility (GEF), the World Bank, and the Asian Development Bank. Bilateral cooperation agreements and memorandums have been signed between China and 42 other countries, including the USA, Japan and Russia. A number of cooperation projects have been implemented in China under bilateral gratis programs from 13 countries and international organizations, including the European Union, Germany and Canada.

Environmental-protection NGOs from various countries, among them the Worldwide Fund for Nature (WWF) and the International Fund for Animal Welfare, have cooperated with Chinese authorities and NGOs with positive results.

Marine Protection

The Law on Protection of the Ocean Environment applies to the supervision and management of the ocean environment; to the surveying, monitoring, assessing and conducting of scientific research of the ocean environment; to construction projects for control of ocean pollution; and to ending ocean dumping pollution. Today, 90 marine nature reserves have been established throughout China. They protect marine shoreline, estuary and island bio-environments, which possess great value for science, education, and natural history; and also protect endangered marine animals such as the Indo-Pacific hump-backed dolphin (*Sousa chinensis*) and their habitats, as well as typical oceanic eco-systems such as mangroves, coral reefs and coastal wetlands. The "Blue Sea Action" program in the Bohai Sea, off the coast of northern China, is one of the country's projects to help clean the ocean.

欧盟—中国科技合作
EU-China Science and Technology Cooperation

Education and Science

孔子学院
Konfuciova akademie
na Univerzitě Palackého

再穷不能穷教育
再苦不能苦孩子

Education System

China has implemented nine-year compulsory education. Preschool education includes kindergartens and other forms; after compulsory education, education includes standard high schools, secondary specialized schools, and higher education includes junior college degrees and above. Moreover, all types of continuing education also exist.

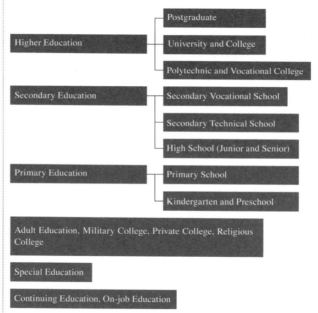

Higher Education
- Postgraduate
- University and College
- Polytechnic and Vocational College

Secondary Education
- Secondary Vocational School
- Secondary Technical School
- High School (Junior and Senior)

Primary Education
- Primary School
- Kindergarten and Preschool

Adult Education, Military College, Private College, Religious College

Special Education

Continuing Education, On-job Education

Tsinghua University

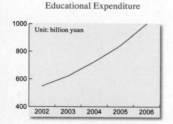

Educational Expenditure

Unit: billion yuan

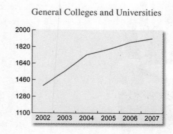

General Colleges and Universities

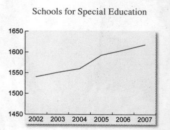

Schools for Special Education

Education Development

China has the world's largest number of people receiving formal education. Over 300 million people are in schools of various kinds. Net elementary school enrollment has reached 99.5%; and gross enrollment rates in junior and senior high schools, and higher-learning institutions are, respectively, 98%, 66% and 23%. Nine-year compulsory education is in effect in over 95% of China's populated areas, with illiteracy in the young and mid-aged population under 4%. Education in China has reached the average level of middle-income countries.

China's educational horizons are expanding, with the number of candidates for master's degrees or higher continuing to soar. The education market has skyrocketed; and training and examination for professional qualifications such as computer and foreign languages are booming. Continuing education is the trend; for the first time, schooling can provide lifelong learning.

Investment in education has increased in recent years, with the proportion of the overall budget allocated to education being raised by over one percentage point annually since 1998. Following a Ministry of Education program, the government will set up an educational financing system that matches the public finance system, emphasizing the

The slogan on the wall says: "Education should not be ignored no matter how poor the village is; children should be well cared for no matter how hard our lives are."

After-class activities

Private Education

The first Law on Promotion of Private Education came into effect on September 1, 2003. Development of private schools means an increase in overall education supply and a change in the traditional pattern of only-government-funded schools to meet the public education needs. By the end of 2007, there were 95,500 private schools of various types and levels, with a total enrollment of 25.83 million, including 295 private schools of higher education and adult colleges.

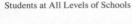

Students at All Levels of Schools

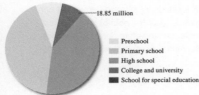

18.85 million

- Preschool
- Primary school
- High school
- College and university
- School for special education

Students Studying Abroad

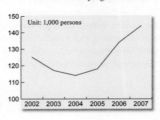

Unit: 1,000 persons

150
140
130
120
110
100
2002 2003 2004 2005 2006 2007

The Number of Students in Non-government-funded Educational Institutions

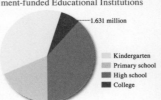

1.631 million

- Kindergarten
- Primary school
- High school
- College

A rural school teacher

The First Primary School in Gyiru Township, Chanang County, Tibet is practicing distant learning by computer.

responsibilities of governments at all levels regarding education funding, and ensuring faster growth of their financial allocations for education compared to regular revenues. The program also expects government education expenditure to expand to 4% of the GDP in as short a period as possible.

For non-compulsory education, China has adopted a shared-cost mechanism, charging tuition at a certain percentage of the cost. To ensure that students from low-income families can receive further education, the government has initiated effective ways of assistance, including scholarships, work-study programs, subsidies for students with special economic difficulties, reduction or exemption of tuition, and state loans.

Special Education

Chinese laws and regulations have defined the right to education of people with disabilities: besides schools for special education, any disabled children capable of adapting to regular study conditions can enroll in standard elementary and high schools. At present, China has 1,618 schools for special education, with 413,000 students; 1,078 vocational education and training institutes for the disabled and 2,257 standard vocational training institutes, admitting 570,000 people with disabilities; and 145 secondary vocational education institutes with 11,259 such students. Since 1979, more than 30,000 people with disabilities have been enrolled in ordinary colleges and universities.

Rural Education

From 2007, the state has exempted rural students from tuition during the compulsory education period. The policy also includes provision of free books and accommodation subsidies to impoverished students.

To implement modern distance-learning projects in rural elementary and middle schools, central and local governments allocated 10 billion yuan for schools in rural areas in central and western China during 2003 to 2007. With this money, junior high schools in rural areas have been equipped with computer rooms; facilities to receive satellite-transmitted teaching programs have been installed in rural elementary schools; and DVD players with complete teaching sets have been supplied to rural elementary teaching centers. Students in rural areas now can enjoy educational resources and IT education that is equal in quality to urban students.

The Central Agricultural Broadcasting and TV School has grown into the world's largest distance education institute for rural areas, with 3,000 branch schools and a staff of 50,000 people. With the help of radio, TV, satellite networks, internet, audio-visual materials and other teaching methods, this school has provided farmers with training in practical technology.

Education Plans

The government is committed to providing more educational opportunities and markedly raising overall educational levels in the next two decades. As targeted in a Ministry of Education program, by 2020, of every 100,000 people, 13,500 will have junior college education or above, and 31,000 will have senior high school education; rates for illiteracy and semi-literacy should fall below 3%; and the national average schooling duration is to be extended from today's 8.5 to nearly 11 years.

China's basic education is expected to approach or attain the levels of moderately developed countries by 2010. In addition, a national program initiated in 1993 is committed to assist 100 universities ascend to world elite ranking within 20 years. For this, a special state fund has been allocated, and so far 30 universities have benefited.

To meet the skyrocketing demand for highly skilled workers, the state is working on two vocational education programs: training personnel urgently needed in modern manufacturing and service industries, and training rural labor migrating to urban areas.

Pupils of a Hope School

Project Hope

"Project Hope," aimed at financing dropout students in poverty-stricken areas to return to school, establishing schools and improving rural educational conditions, is a social public welfare program, carried out by the China Youth Development Foundation since 1989. Donations to establish Project Hope schools and financing poor students are the two major programs of Project Hope.

In 18 years, over 3.5 billion yuan have been raised by Project Hope, to finance more than 2.9 million impoverished students, establish over 13,000 Project Hope schools as well as over 13,000 Hope reading rooms and libraries, and train more than 35,000 rural teachers.

On May 20, 2007, Project Hope shifted from its "rescue one child" mode toward "rescue plus development," paying more attention to impoverished students' potential for self-improvement. Furthermore, Project Hope also added more financial programs, e.g., work-study and social practice, etc., for all assisted students on the basis of existing stipends.

International Exchanges of Education

China is seeing active cooperation and exchanges in education with the rest of the world. Exchange students are a major part in this regard, and no other country has more people studying abroad than China. Since 1979, over 1,000,000 Chinese have studied in over 100 countries and regions, of whom nearly 300,000 have returned after finishing their studies. The number of foreign students in China has also increased rapidly. Since 1979, over 1,026,000 students from 188 countries studied at 544 Chinese universities.

Today, learning Chinese language has become a popular pursuit around the world. Since 2004, China has opened not-for-profit Confucius Institutes overseas, with the aim of spreading Chinese language and culture. So far, 226 Confucius institutes and schools have been established in 64 countries and regions. Over 40 million people overseas are learning Chinese through various ways. Over 8,000 schools in nearly 100 countries have set Chinese language in their curricula.

The Confucius Institute established at Palacky University, Olomouc, Czech, on September 26, 2007

The 13th China International Education Fair held in Beijing, March 2008

Science and Technology

A hundred years ago, China had no modern science and technology at all — fewer than 10 people in the country understood calculus. But by the early 21st century, the high-tech research and development gap between China and the world's advanced countries has shrunk visibly; 60% of China's technologies, including atomic energy, space, high-energy physics, biosciences, computer and information technology and robotics, have reached or are close to advanced world levels. The successful launches of manned spacecraft in 2003 and 2005 marked a leap in Chinese astronautics. Following its successful Moon Probe Project in 2007, China plans to launch unmanned probes to the moon before 2010, and gather moon soil samples before 2020.

A Motorola workshop in Tianjin

The Law on Progress of Science and Technology, promulgated in 1993, provides basic guidance for China's scientific and technological development. It clarifies the goal and role of development, funding sources and awards regarding scientific and technological achievements. The Law on Popularization of Science and Technology, promulgated in 2002, makes it a societal goal to popularize science and technology among all citizens. Local regulations have been issued for attracting talented people, ensuring investment in science and technology, and developing high technology.

In February 2006, the State Council issued its Guidelines for the National Medium- and Long-term Program for Science and Technology Development (2006-2020). This outlines a plan to speed up research in 16 major or key technologies in the next 15 years, covering strategic industries such as information and biosciences; important and urgent issues concerning energy, resources, environment and health; and also R&D in large aircraft, manned space flight and the Moon Probe Project. By 2020, China's overall investment in research and experiments is expected to top 2.5% of its GDP, compared with 1.33% in 2005; the progress of science and technology will contribute over 60% to China's development.

R&D Expenditure

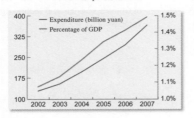

Corresponding Full-time Staff in R&D

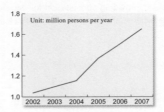

China and the European Union have enhanced cooperation in science and technology fields.

A lab in Nankai University's Teda Applied Physics School

Innovations of Science and Technology

In the 21st century, China is enhancing the capability of independent innovation as the basic strategy of its science and technology development. Governments at all levels have provided strong financial support toward independent innovations. In 2007, the state allocated 168.9 billion yuan for science and technology, which accounts for the largest proportion of national fiscal expenditure since 1998, an increase of 26.5% over the previous year.

Many of China's agricultural science and technology results are leading the world, among them bird-flu vaccine, insect-resistant cotton, dwarf-male-sterile wheat, super-high-yield rice, and low-erucic-acid and low-glucosinolate oilseed. China has also developed and applied a wealth of key generic technologies in precision manufacturing, clean energy, intelligent communications and information security; and made breakthroughs in core technologies significant to urban environmental pollution control, resource exploration and utilization, natural-disaster alleviation and prevention, and ecological protection. It has also achieved many innovative successes in frontier fields such as micro-electronic materials, photo-electronic materials, functional ceramics, nano-materials, and bio-medical materials.

CAS and CAE

The Chinese Academy of Sciences (CAS) is China's highest academic institute and comprehensive research center in natural sciences. Its academic divisions include mathematics, physics, chemistry, geography, biology and technological sciences; and it has more than 100 subordinate research institutes across the country, including 30 internationally prestigious ones. The Chinese Academy of Engineering (CAE) is the highest honorary consultative institute in engineering science and technology, conducting strategic studies of the state's important engineering-related issues and providing consultation for decision-making. The CAS has 736 academicians, and the CAE, 737. Both also have foreign academicians.

Sci-tech Human Resources

China has 35 million scientific and technological personnel, the most in the world, and 1.65 million of them are engaged full-time in sci-tech R&D, ranking second in the world. Of the winners of national sci-tech awards in 2007, 61% were under 45, the age group who has become the mainstay of China's science and technology development.

International Cooperation

China has developed its sci-tech cooperation with 152 countries and regions, signing intergovernmental sci-tech cooperation agreements with 96 of them, and joined more than 1,000 international sci-tech cooperation organizations. Non-governmental, international sci-tech cooperation and exchange have been most active. The China Association for Science and Technology and its affiliated organizations have joined 249 international scientific and technological organizations; for a total of 373 times, the Chinese have held executive member/directorship of executive councils or boards of directors, or higher, in such organizations; and for 280 times, they have held leading posts on related special committees; and more than 250 CAS scientists hold posts in international scientific organizations. The China National Science Foundation has concluded cooperative agreements and memoranda with counterpart organizations in 36 countries.

Awards for International Scientific and Technological Cooperation, national prizes established by the State Council, are granted to foreign scientists, engineers, managers or organizations for their contribution to China's bilateral or multilateral sci-tech cooperation. By 2007, 44 foreigners had won the honor.

Social Sciences

China has more than 100,000 researchers engaged in social sciences. The Chinese Academy of Social Sciences (CASS), established in 1977, is the top academic organization in the field, by virtue of its comprehensive scope and concentration of human talent, data and research materials. It is known for creative theoretical exploration and policy research. The Academy has 36 institutes with over 3,400 researchers, some 2,000 of them senior experts, including many well known in international academic circles, or younger and middle-age researchers distinguishing themselves in theoretical studies.

In August 2006, the CASS established five academic divisions: literature, history and philosophy; economics; social politics and law; international research; and Marxism. It has 47 ordinary and 95 honorary members with academic status equivalent to that of CAS academicians.

China attaches importance to international exchanges in traditional Chinese medicine (TCM) with science and technology. The photo shows the "Summit on TCM Modernization."

China prioritizes international high-tech cooperation. The picture shows the Hanwang Technology Co. signing a cooperation agreement with Israel's WizCom Technologies Ltd.

A reader in a bookstore in Nanjing

Top 10 Sci-tech Advances in 2007

In early 2008, China's Top 10 Scientific and Technological Advances of 2007, as voted by 547 CAS and CAE academicians, were unveiled:

The successful launching of the Chang'e-1 moon probe satellite, with clear moon surface images obtained — ranking China among the few countries with deep-space exploration capabilities.

China's first 12,000m ultra-deep drilling rig developed with independent IPR — upgrading China's exploration in deep terrestrial and marine oil and gas fields.

Great progress in research on cancer treatment — Chinese researchers' published findings on nano-micelles, delivering chemotherapeutic drugs directly to cancer cells, and research report on the discovery of a new target for cancer treatment — both published in internationally respected medical journals.

Six-atom Schrodinger "cat" state achieved — researchers in China's National Laboratory have successfully created a six-atom Schrodinger "cat" state, enabling the highest atom-entanglement in the world, with the cluster state directly used for quantum computation, setting new records in the fields of atom-entanglement and quantum computation.

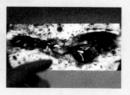

Fossils of dormant animal eggs from 632 million years ago discovered — pushing animal fossil records back 50 million years.

The first domestically developed regional plane, the ARJ21 rolled out of workshop — marking China's development of new regional aircraft, joining ranks of world civilian aircraft.

The world's largest bird-like beast-footed dinosaur — fossils of a giant theropod, the world's largest bird-like beast-footed dinosaur, found in Erenhot, Inner Mongolia.

Breakdown of the Born-Oppenheimer Approximation in the interaction of fluorine and deuterium atoms discovered — a significant academic breakthrough in kinetics studies of non-adiabatic process.

China's first wildlife germplasm bank built in Yunnan — with seed bank, in-vitro plant germplasm resource bank, DNA bank, microbial seed bank, animal germplasm resource bank, information center, and plant germplasm resource field.

Record of high-yield new soybean variety — 371.8 kg/*mu* (15 *mu*=1 ha), also the highest record for soybean production in China in the new century.

Life and Culture

Social Life

Sports and Physical Fitness

Culture and Arts

Mass Media

Social Life

Income and Consumption

China-made Dongfeng family wagon

According to figures released by the National Bureau of Statistics of China, the average per-capita disposable income of urban residents in 2007 amounted to 13,786 yuan, and the average per-capita net income of rural residents was 4,140 yuan. In 2007, China's per-capita GDP exceeded US$ 2,000. Today, China's consumers are spending their money on education, housing, automobiles, computers, stocks, and overseas travel. Living conditions have likewise further improved. Clothing, food, housing and transportation show the greatest changes, reflecting greater interest in fashion, nutrition and home comfort. Traveling by taxi or in one's own car has become commonplace.

The Engel coefficient (food expenses as a percentage of total consumer spending) fell from 39.4% in 2000 to 36.3% in 2007, according to data from the National Bureau of Statistics. The figure is gradually approaching developed countries' figures of around 30%; while among rural households it fell from 49.1% to 43.1%.

Private Cars

According to data from the National Bureau of Statistics of China, the number of private vehicles in the country is increasing at an average annual rate of 20%, surpassing economic growth. By the end of 2007, the number of private vehicles in China reached 35.34 million, of which 15.22 million were private cars. In 2007, on average about 6.1 automobiles were owned per 100 urban households.

Housing

In terms of newly built housing, the present percentage of individual housing purchase is 93%. In view of the housing stockpile, the percentage of residents owning their home has reached around 80%, basically forming an urban housing ownership structure with a large proportion of individual ownership. According to data of the National Bureau of Statistics, in 2006, the area of newly built urban housing was 630 million sq m, with average individual living area at 27.1 sq m; the figure for newly built rural housing was 684 million sq m, with average individual living area being 30.7 sq m.

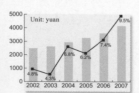

Rural Per-capita Net Income

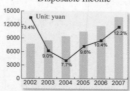

Urban Residents' Per-capita Disposable Income

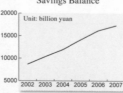

Urban Residents' Total Savings Balance

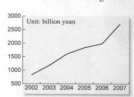

Total Personal Housing Loans

What are people doing on the Internet?

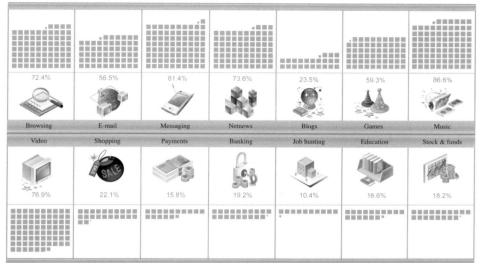

Browsing	E-mail	Messaging	Netnews	Blogs	Games	Music
72.4%	56.5%	81.4%	73.6%	23.5%	59.3%	86.6%

Video	Shopping	Payments	Banking	Job hunting	Education	Stock & funds
76.9%	22.1%	15.8%	19.2%	10.4%	16.6%	18.2%

What do people own in their households?

	Color TV	Fridge	Washing machine	Air-conditioner	Mobile phone	Computer
Rural areas	94.4%	26.1%	45.9%	8.5%	77.8%	3.7%
Urban areas	137.8%	95.0%	96.8%	95.1%	165.2%	53.8%

Per-capita Housing Area

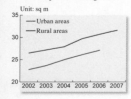

Unit: sq m
— Urban areas
— Rural areas

Number of Private Cars in China

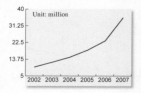

Unit: million

Unemployment Rate in Selected Countries

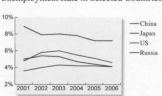

— China
— Japan
— US
— Russia

Employment

Every year, China has a large number of newly emerged urban workers, laid-off workers and surplus rural labor. While continuing to implement positive employment policies and to increase employment and re-employment opportunities, the government is speeding up progress on a social insurance system that protects people's interests and helps build a harmonious society. From 2006 to 2010, China will annually provide new work for at least 9 million people in urban areas, with the rate of registered unemployment to be restricted to under 5%. In 2007, China provided jobs for 12.04 million people in urban areas, with a registered unemployment rate of 4%.

The First Community of Zhongyuan Oilfield of Henan helping find jobs for disabled people

Social Security

The Chinese government proposed that by 2020 it will have basically built a social security system for urban and rural residents; with about one fifth of the world's population, by then it should have the world's largest social security system.

Minimum Standard of Living

A minimum-standard-of-living system has been established in all cities and county towns, providing basic guarantees for residents with family per-capita income below the minimum local standard. In 2007, there were 22.71 million urban residents receiving such living-standard support, and all low-income people meeting the requirements are covered by insurance. The system is being set up in many rural areas.

Rural Cooperative Medical-care System

In 2003, China embarked on a new rural cooperative medical-care system. Focused on major-illness health insurance coverage, the system is based on a payment plan from individuals, financial support from the collective, and subsidies from the government. If a farmer who has joined the scheme is hospitalized, some incurred costs can be reimbursed according to a sliding scale. This medical-care system is expected to cover the whole country by 2010. Meanwhile, China has implemented a medical-aid system for rural areas, offering free medical aid to poor farmers who are seriously ill. A standardized rural medical-aid system has been established throughout the country. The funds, raised from special allocations from various levels of government and from voluntary donations from society, will be used exclusively for free medical aid.

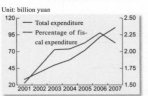

Total Expenditure in Civil Administration

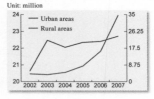

Number of People Receiving Minimum Standard of Living

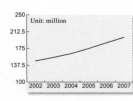

Number of People Having Old-age Insurance

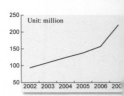

Number of People Covered by Basic Medical Insurance

Senior citizens waiting to apply for social security and pension at a local security office in Zheng-zhou, Henan Province

As a populous developing country, it is not easy for China to catch up with advanced countries in terms of its current levels of social security, which can guarantee only basic living standards for its citizens. Its standards cover three aspects: pension insurance, maintaining a moderate living standard for workers after retirement; unemployment insurance, maintaining subsistence for workers in case of unemployment; and medical insurance, covering ordinary medical demands for the insured. Since the 1990s, China has actively pursued reforms of its old-age, unemployment and medical insurance systems. The State Council promulgated Regulations on Unemployment Insurance, Interim Regulations on the Collection of Social Insurance Premiums, and Regulations on Guaranteeing Urban Residents' Minimum Standard of Living, providing legal guarantees for the implementation of the social security system. Now, quite separate from enterprises and institutions, a social security system managed by the society is taking shape, which integrates old-age, unemployment and medical insurances, as well as minimum living standards. By the end of August in 2007, the Chinese government has accumulated over 360 billion

Number of People Covered
by Unemployment Insurance

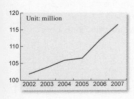

Number of People Covered by
Occupational Injury Insurance

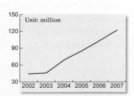

Number of People Covered by
Maternity Insurance

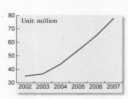

Number of People Covered by
New-type Rural Cooperative
Medical Care Insurance

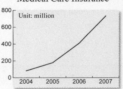

yuan for national social security funds through various channels, including fiscal allotment.

From only state- and collective-owned enterprises, social insurance coverage has expanded to non-public enterprises and institutions, as well as those who are flexibly employed. By the end of 2007, 201.07 million people had participated in basic old-age insurance, 220.51 million in medical insurance, and 116.45 million in unemployment insurance.

Health and Medical Care

People's Hospital, Beijing

For every 1,000 people, China has 1.56 doctors and 2.63 hospital beds. In Beijing, Shanghai, Tianjin, Chongqing and other large cities, general hospitals and hospitals specializing in areas such as cancer, cardio- and cerebro-vascular disorders, ophthalmology, dentistry and infectious diseases can be found. Medium-sized cities throughout China have general and specialized hospitals with modern facilities. Medical treatment, disease prevention, and healthcare networks have taken shape at county, township and village

Traditional Chinese Medicine

Compared with Western medicine, traditional Chinese medicine (TCM) has its independent theory and diagnostic methods such as observation, pulse-taking and acupuncture, with herbal medicine as its main treatment. Its unique medical effects have long been acknowledged through clinical practice. At present, China has over 3,000 hospitals adopting traditional Chinese medicine, with nearly 300,000 hospital beds and a related staff of more than 500,000 practicing doctors, including assistant TCM-practicing doctors. Most general hospitals have set up TCM departments. In cities, 90% of community medical centers offer TCM services; in the countryside, about 70% of counties have TCM hospitals, 75% of township hospitals have TCM departments, and 40% of village doctors treat patients by adopting traditional Chinese medicine or integrating it with Western medicine.

Integrating Traditional Chinese Medicine and Western Medicine

Medical technology commonly applied worldwide, referred to by the Chinese as "Western medicine," is found throughout the country and available through relatively high-level clinical treatment. Today, both TCM and Western medicine are being used by China's medical professionals, particularly in effective ways to diagnose and cure difficult and complicated cases. Such integration has combined both of their features and advantages in disease diagnosis and treatment. So far, there are 167 hospitals providing treatment by integrating TCM and Western medicine, with a related staff over 40,000. Integrated medical treatment has also been offered by most general hospitals. In order to find more optimal ways for such integration, the state has provided tremendous support in building 27 specialized departments and 11 hospitals, all providing combined treatment.

levels. With the establishment and development of health and medical-care organizations, along with the steady spread of better hygiene habits, infectious and parasitic diseases that were formerly major killers have been replaced by cancer, cardio- and cerebro-vascular diseases, creating a mortality pattern closer to that of the developed countries. The health of urban and rural residents has been greatly improved; the average life expectancy is now 73.0 years, close to the levels of intermediate developed countries.

"Prevention first" is one of the important principles in all healthcare work in China. All administrative levels have established hygiene and disease-prevention organizations responsible for overall management of these functions including hygiene and epidemic prevention stations, forming a nationwide network of hygiene supervision and control. In May 2003, the State Council issued its Regulations on Public Health Emergency Responses, establishing a legal framework for tackling public-health crises.

TCM pharmacists dispensing traditional medicine to patients

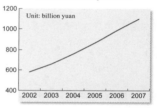

Total Health Expenditure

Different types of medical insurance systems are being carried out in urban and rural areas.

The National Grand Theater

Sports and Physical Fitness

Mass Sports

Table tennis is very popular among people in China.

There are an extreme abundance of physical forms of exercise and 850,000 sports sites nationwide. There are 6.58 sports sites for every 10,000 people, with a sports site area per capita of 1.03 sq m. A survey released by the General Administration of Sports of China indicates that more than 60% of urban residents in China go to sports clubs for physical fitness activities, and over 95% of students have attained the National Physical Exercise Standard.

Nationwide Physical Fitness Program

Public fitness facilities in a residential community

The Physical Health Law of the People's Republic of China was adopted in 1995. In the same year, the State Council promulgated its "Outline for a Nationwide Physical Fitness Program," followed by a series of rules and regulations. The Nationwide Physical Fitness Program has set targets for 2010, that more than 40% of China's population should participate in regular physical exercises, with clear improvement in national physical health and a major increase in the number of fitness sites, so as to satisfy people's needs to keep fit.

Aiming to improve the health and physical condition of the general population, the Nationwide Physical Fitness Program, with an emphasis on youth and children, encourages everyone to engage in at least one sports activity every day, learn at least two ways of keeping fit, and have a health examination every year.

Welfare Lottery

Unit: billion yuan

— Total sales
— Utilized for public welfare funds

80
60
40
20
0
2002 2003 2004 2005 2006 2007

Sports Lotteries and Physical Fitness Facilities

The government has stipulated that 60% of the proceeds from sports lotteries must go to the nationwide physical fitness program. By the end of 2006, the General Administration of Sports of China had constructed about 6,000 physical fitness projects throughout rural and urban areas nationwide, using the lottery proceeds. Starting from 2001, the Administration began to earmark lottery money as pilot funds to build "China Sports Lottery Nationwide Physical Fitness Centers," as pilot projects in 31 large and medium-sized cities throughout China, including Dalian, Beijing and Changchun, some already in use. Meanwhile, about 196 million yuan of sports lottery proceeds were used to construct public sporting facilities in China's less-developed western areas and the Yangtze Three Gorges region, benefiting 101 counties and towns.

Taiji Fan performance

In this 15-year-long program, the government aims to build a sports and fitness service system for the general public. Most gymnasiums and stadiums across China are open to and widely used by the general public. Outdoor fitness centers have been installed in urban communities, public parks, squares, roadsides and other convenient locations, equipped with various forms of fitness equipment and facilities.

Sports Meet

Five large-scale sports competitions are held at regular intervals in China, including the National Games, National Farmers' Games, National University Games, National Games for the Disabled, and National Minorities Traditional Sports Games, to promote sports development nationwide.

The National Games, held once every four years, are comprehensive athletic games at the highest level, held 10 times to date. The National Farmers' Games, which is held once every four years, has been held five times. The National University Games, which is held once every four years, aimed at inspecting the health conditions of students in universities, has been held eight times. The National Games for the Disabled, which is held once every four years, has been held six times. In November 1953, the first National Minorities Traditional Sports Games was held, aimed at presenting distinctive traditional sports and setting competitive standards for folk sports; it has since been held eight times.

Exercising in fitness centers has become fashionable among young people.

A Canoe Kayak-Slalom competition in Beijing's Olympic Rowing-Canoeing Park

Traditional Sports

Traditional sports with distinct Chinese characteristics are also very popular, including martial arts, *taijiquan*, *qigong*, Chinese chess, and *weiqi* or go.

Children practicing martial arts

Martial arts (*wushu*) combine exercise with arts of self-defense. They include bare-fist boxing as well as the use of offensive and defensive apparatus, with different schools and moves. *Taijiquan*, or Chinese shadow-boxing, emphasizes body movement following mind movement, tempering robustness with gentleness and graceful postures. A system of deep breathing exercises, *qigong* is a unique Chinese way of keeping fit, aimed at enhancing health, prolonging life, treating illness and improving physiological functions, by focusing the mind and regulating breathing.

There are also a variety of entertaining and competitive sports activities in minority areas, for example, wrestling and horsemanship of the Mongol, Uygur and Kazak people; Tibetan yak racing; Korean "seesaw jumping;" Miao crossbow; and the dragon-boat racing of the Dai.

Liu Xiang, China's champion of men's 110m hurdle at the Athens Olympic Games

Competitive Sports

Back in March 1959, at the 25th World Table Tennis Championships held in Germany, table-tennis player Rong Guotuan won the first world title in China's sporting history. By the end of 2007, Chinese athletes had altogether won 2,170 world championships and broken world records 1,175 times. In the 19 years since 1989, Chinese athletes have won 1,816 world championships, accounting for 83.7% of the total; and have broken 793 world records, accounting for 67.5% of total new records set. It was a period when China's competitive sports enjoyed continuous and rapid development.

In the new century, Chinese young athletes have begun to demonstrate increasing maturity on the world stage. Hurdler Liu Xiang, basketball player Yao Ming and Yi Jianlian, rowers Meng Guanliang and Yang Wenjun, tennis players Sun Tiantian, Li Ting, Yan Zi and Zheng Jie, snooker player Ding Junhui are all examples of top-class athletes.

Yao Ming, world-famous Chinese basketball star in the NBA

The credit for China's achievements in competitive sports should go to its training system, which is constantly being perfected. It has its base in the juvenile amateur sports schools and basic-level clubs, with teams representing localities as the backbone, and the national team at the highest level. The training system ensures that China's elite teams maintain a year-round squad of about 20,000 outstanding athletes. On February 3, 2004, the State Council proclaimed its Anti-Doping Regulations, the first detailed stipulations concerning the control of performance-enhancing drugs, anti-doping obligations, examination and monitoring, and legal liabilities. The Regulations came into force on March 1, 2004.

Sports for People with Disabilities

Chinese sports for the disabled play a leading role in the world and have won many excellent achievements in world-class competitions. The Chinese Paralympics team initially entered the ranks of the top ten at the Atlanta Paralympics in 1996, the top six at Sydney in 2000, and led the medals at the Athens Paralympics in 2004. By 2006, Chinese disabled athletes had taken home 2,072 gold medals and set or broken world records on 214 occasions.

People in wheelchairs participating in a race

The establishment of the National Paralympics Committee of China in 1983 institutionalized Chinese sports for people with disabilities. The China Sports Association for the Deaf and Special Olympics China were established in 1985 and 1986, respectively; and sports associations for people with disabilities in each province, autonomous region and municipality have been set up. China has already joined eight comprehensive international sports organizations for people with disabilities, as well as dozens of international organizations for particular sports. Shanghai was qualified to host the 2007 Special Olympics International, while Beijing will host the 2008 Paralympics Games.

Jin Jing, Chinese Paralympic fencer, and famed torch bearer for the 2008 Olympics

Culture and Arts

Libraries

By the end of 2007, China had 2,791 public libraries, with collections exceeding 500 million volumes. University and college library collections are led by Peking and Wuhan universities. The national library network also includes libraries of scientific research institutions, various primary-level entities, and elementary and high schools.

The National Library

The Palace Museum, Beijing

The National Library of China, with a collection of 25 million volumes, is the largest in Asia and holds the world's largest collection of books in Chinese. Among its huge collection are more than 3,500 ancient tortoiseshells carved with Chinese pictographs, 1.6 million volumes of ancient thread-bound books, some 1,000 volumes of documents from the Dunhuang Grottoes, 12 million foreign-language books and magazines, and dozens of electronic databases. The library began to accept submissions of official publications in 1916 and began to accept domestic electronic publications in 1987. It is also China's ISSN (International Standard Serial Number) Center and Network Information Center. The library has formed a digital library alliance with 90 other libraries across the country to promote China's digital public information service. The second phase of the National Library, the China Digital Library, is now under construction. The project is expected to satisfy book storage demand for the next 30 years. The Digital Library will make the National Library the world's largest Chinese literature collection center and digital resource base, as well as the most advanced information network service base in China.

The Shanghai Library is China's largest provincial-level library. It has a collection of over 1.7 million volumes of ancient documents, among which 25,000 titles of rare books in 178,000 volumes are the most valuable, many being the only surviving copies anywhere; the earliest document dates back nearly 1,500 years.

Museums

There are 1,634 museums in China. Including certain non-governmental museums with special features, the total number of museums of various kinds comes to more than 2,400. With a total collection surpassing 20 million items, these museums hold nearly 10,000 exhibitions a year. Museums based on cultural relics, like the Museum of the Qin Terracotta Warriors and Horses in Xi'an, have attracted countless tourists both at home and abroad. The Chinese government encourages exchanges and exhibitions of cultural relics between museums, as well as the display and exchange of legitimate private collections. By 2015, China will build 1,000 additional museums, so that every city of medium size or larger will possess at least one comprehensive museum.

Flanking the eastern side of Tiananmen Square in Beijing, the National Museum of China integrates a variety of functions of archeological study, collection, research and display, and possesses more than 600,000 items (or sets) of precious ancient, modern and contemporary Chinese cultural relics as well as millions of literary documents. The museum's expansion project is scheduled to be completed by 2010, expanding its area to 192,000 sq m.

Preservation of Cultural Relics

China has nearly 400,000 known unmovable cultural relics above ground or underground. A total of 2,351 cultural sites are under national protection. There are over 7,000 cultural sites under provincial-level protection and more than 60,000 under municipal- and county-level protection. The national database for information on cultural relics will be completed and open to the public by 2015.

In the 1990s, China made significant investments in protecting and rescuing cultural relics. Special Central Government subsidies for the protection of cultural relics totaled over 700 million yuan for more than 1,000 projects. As a result, large numbers of cultural relics were saved from destruction. According to a program launched in 2005, the state will provide 250 million yuan yearly to the protection of key relics nationwide.

Cultural relics have come under increasing legal protection. China has signed four international treaties on relics preservation. The Law on the Protection of Cultural Relics, promulgated in 1982, institutes clear regulations on immovable cultural relics, archeological excavations, cultural relics preserved in museums, folk cultural relics, and the import

"Terracotta Army," in the mausoleum of the First Emperor of the Qin Dynasty (221-206 BC)

Hall of Supreme Harmony in the Imperial Palace, Beijing

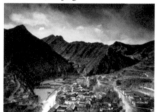

Cuandixia village, a venerable village built during the Ming and Qing dynasties

and export of cultural relics, etc. Implementation Regulations for the Law on the Protection of Cultural Relics and Provisional Regulations on the Administration of Auction of Relics were issued in 2003. In 2006, Measures of Beijing Municipality on the Protection of the Great Wall, the first such special regulations, came into effect.

By the end of 2007, the Chinese government had listed 110 famous historical and cultural cities under key national protection and over 80 under provincial-level protection. From 2001, an annual 15 million yuan has been allocated for their protection.

As a large traditionally agricultural country, China has a vast range of ancient villages, a rare phenomenon in the world. Their natural environment, as well as folk customs and handicrafts have been well preserved. The State Administration of Cultural Heritage is planning a major ancient village protection project; and at the end of 2007, released the names of 85 towns and 72 villages under special protection.

The Temple of Heaven, Beijing

Intangible Cultural Heritage

China possesses a great number of intangible cultural heritage, one of the world's richest. In June 2006, China promulgated the first catalogue of state-level intangible cultural heritage, which includes 518 items in 10 categories – folk literature, folk music, folk dance, traditional drama, opera, acrobatics and competitive sports, folk art, traditional handicraft, traditional medicine, and folk customs.

China's Kunqu Opera, and the art of playing the *guqin* (seven-stringed zither), Uygur Muqam music and Mongolian pastoral songs have been included on the UNESCO list of Masterpieces of Oral and Intangible Heritage of Humanity. In 2005, for the first time, China submitted a joint application with another country (Mongolia) for Mongolian pastoral songs to be entered on the list. In addition, the Chinese traditional music sound archives, the records of the Qing-dynasty Grand Secretariat, the list of successful candidates in the Qing Dynasty (1644-1911) imperial examinations, the ancient Naxi Dongba literature manuscripts and Qing-dynasty architectural design archives of the Lei family have also been inscribed on the Memory of the World program. In 2001, the Chinese Tibetan epic *King Gesar*, the world's longest epic, was listed by UNESCO in the world millennium memorials.

China has carried out a great deal of effective work on the protection of intangible cultural heritage, including *Ten Collections on China's Folk and Minority Cultures and Arts*, a compilation of 300 volumes of nearly 500 million words, organized by the government for the purpose of protecting precious art and cultural resources. In February 2006, the State Council promulgated its Notice on Intensifying the Protection of Intangible Cultural Heritage, giving detailed requirements for its survey, protection and rescue, establishing a regional listing at all levels, and ultimately forming a national system to protect intangible cultural heritage.

Beijing opera facial makeup

Tiger hat

Dragon dance

Paper-cut

Natural and Cultural Heritage

The Kaiping Watchtowers (*diaolou*), with their surrounding villages in Guangdong Province, and China Karsts were placed on the World Heritage list, at the 31st session of the World Heritage Committee of the United Nations Educational, Scientific and Cultural Organization (UNESCO) held in June 2007. These unique watchtowers found throughout Kaiping, Guangdong, are multi-storied defensive buildings. Along with their villages, they embody architectural and design combinations between China and the West from the 19th century. China Karst consists of typical Chinese karst topography areas, including pinnacle, pillar-shaped and pagoda-shaped karsts in Shilin (stone forest), Yunnan Province, pyramidal-shaped karsts in Libo, Guizhou Province, and the *Difeng* (earth fissures) and *Tiankeng* (pits) areas in Wulong, Chongqing Municipality. They were formed 500,000 to 300 million years ago, with a total area of 1,460 sq km.

Since joining the Convention Concerning the Protection of World Cultural and Natural Heritage in 1985, China now has 35 World Heritage Sites, ranking third in the world. Since 2004, massive renovations have been made to Beijing's six cultural heritage sites — the Ming Tombs, the Great Wall, the Forbidden City, the Temple of Heaven, the Summer Palace, and the Peking Man Site at Zhoukoudian, all planned for completion by 2008. Beginning in 2006, China set the second Saturday of June to be its Cultural Heritage Day.

Sketch Map Showing Distribution of Natural and Cultural Heritage Sites

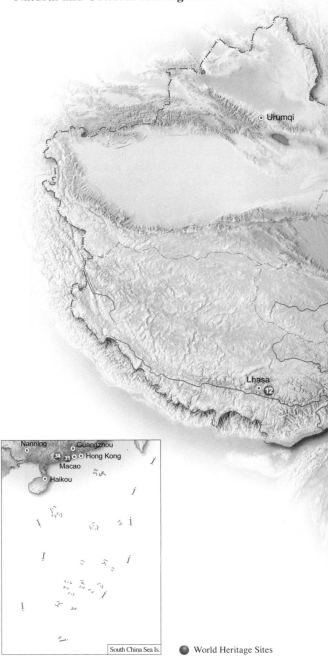

Harbin

Changchun

Shenyang ② ㉔

㉚

Hohhot

⑪

㉘ Beijing ★ ㉔

㉔ Tianjin

Yinchuan

Taiyuan ⑰ Shijiazhuang

Xining   Jinan ⑥

Lanzhou   ㉜   ⑬

Xi'an ⑤ ㉕ Zhengzhou

⑧ ⑨

⑭   Nanjing

Hefei ㉔ ⑱ Shanghai

㉝   Wuhan ㉔   ⑦

㉖ Chengdu   ㉗ Hangzhou

Chongqing ㉓ ㉟

⑯   ⑩   ⑮

Changsha   Nanchang

㉒

⑲   Fuzhou   Taibei

Guiyang ㉟

Kunming ㉟

Nanning   Guangzhou

㉞ Macao Hong Kong

㉛

Haikou

Legend markers (upper left):
① ② ③ ⑳ ㉑ ㉔

1. The Great Wall
(Beijing, 1987, World Cultural Heritage)

2. Imperial Palaces of the Ming and Qing Dynasties in Beijing and Shenyang
(World Cultural Heritage: the Forbidden City, Beijing, 1987;
Imperial Palace of the Qing Dynasty, Shenyang, Liaoning
Province, 2004)

3. Peking Man Site at Zhoukoudian
(Beijing, 1987, World Cultural Heritage)

4. Mogao Caves
(Gansu Province, 1987, World Cultural Heritage)

5. Mausoleum of the First Qin Emperor
(Shaanxi Province, 1987, World Cultural Heritage)

6. Mount Taishan
(Shandong Province, 1987, World Cultural and Natural Heritage)

7. Mount Huangshan
(Anhui Province, 1990, World Cultural and Natural Heritage)

8. Jiuzhaigou Valley Scenic and Historic Interest Area
(Sichuan Province, 1992, World Natural Heritage)

9. Huanglong Scenic and Historic Interest Area
(Sichuan Province, 1992, World Natural Heritage)

10. Wulingyuan Scenic and Historic Interest Area
(Hunan Province, 1992, World Natural Heritage)

11. Mountain Resort and Its Outlying Temples, Chengde
(Hebei Province, 1994, World Cultural Heritage)

12. Historic Ensemble of the Potala Palace, Lhasa
(Tibet Autonomous Region, 1994, World Cultural Heritage)

13. Temple and Cemetery of Confucius and the Kong Family Mansion in Qufu
(Shandong Province, 1994, World Cultural Heritage)

14. Ancient Building Complex in the Wudang Mountains
(Hubei Province, 1994, World Cultural Heritage)

15. Lushan National Park
(Jiangxi Province, 1996, World Cultural Heritage)

16. Mount Emei Scenic Area, Including Leshan Giant Buddha Scenic Area
(Sichuan Province, 1996, World Cultural and Natural Heritage)

17. Ancient City of Pingyao
(Shanxi Province, 1997, World Cultural Heritage)

18. Classical Gardens of Suzhou
(Jiangsu Province, 1997, World Cultural Heritage)

19. Old Town of Lijiang

(Yunnan Province, 1997, World Cultural Heritage)

20. Summer Palace, an Imperial Garden in Beijing

(Beijing, 1998, World Cultural Heritage)

21. Temple of Heaven, an Imperial Sacrificial Altar in Beijing

(Beijing, 1998, World Cultural Heritage)

22. Mount Wuyi

(Fujian Province, 1999, World Cultural and Natural Heritage)

23. Dazu Rock Carvings

(Chongqing, 1999, World Cultural Heritage)

24. Imperial Mausoleums of the Ming and Qing Dynasties

(World Cultural Heritage: Ming Xianling Mausoleum, Hubei Province, 2000;
Qing Dongling Mausoleum and Qing Xiling Mausoleum, Hebei Province, 2000;

Ming Tombs, Beijing, 2003;

Ming Xiaoling Mausoleum, Jiangsu, 2003;

three imperial mausoleums of Shengjing, Liaoning Province, 2004)

25. Longmen Grottoes

(Henan Province, 2000, World Cultural Heritage)

26. Mount Qingcheng and the Dujiangyan Irrigation System

(Sichuan Province, 2000, World Cultural Heritage)

27. Ancient Villages in Southern Anhui — Xidi and

Hongcun

(Anhui Province, 2000, World Cultural Heritage)

28. Yungang Grottoes

(Shanxi Province, 2001, World Cultural Heritage)

29. Three Parallel Rivers of Yunnan Protected Areas

(Yunnan Province, 2003, World Natural Heritage)

30.Capital Cities and Tombs of the Ancient Koguryo

Kingdom

(Liaoning and Jilin Provinces, 2004, World Cultural Heritage)

31. Historic Center of Macao

(Macao Special Administrative Region, 2005, World Cultural Heritage)

32. Yin Xu

(Henan Province, 2006, World Cultural Heritage)

33. Sichuan Giant Panda Sanctuaries

(Sichuan Province, 2006, World Natural Heritage)

34. Kaiping Diaolou and Villages

(Guangdong Province, 2007, World Cultural Heritage)

35. South China Karst

(Yunnan Province, Guizhou Province and Chongqing Municipality, 2007, World Natural Heritage)

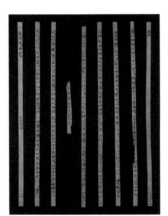

Inscribed bamboo-slips, the oldest writing material in China.

A Dream of Red Mansions, Three Kingdoms, Journey to the West and *Outlaws of the Marsh* are considered the four famous classic novels in China.

Literature

The Book of Songs, China's first anthology of poems and earliest literary achievement, was compiled in the 6th century BC. Literature of the long succession of dynasties that followed includes pre-Qin prose in a simple style, magnificent Han-dynasty *fu* (rhymed prose), and *yuefu* (folksongs) of the late Han. The Tang Dynasty alone can be credited with hundreds of poets, including Li Bai, Du Fu and Bai Juyi, who left more than 50,000 enduring poems. The Song Dynasty was known for its *ci* (lyrics), and the Yuan Dynasty for *zaju* (poetic drama set to music). The Ming and Qing dynasties saw the production of four masterpiece novels: *Three Kingdoms*, *Outlaws of the Marsh*, *Journey to the West* and *A Dream of Red Mansions*. These classics have been celebrated for centuries for their rich historical and cultural connotations and unique styles.

The development of modern Chinese literature has seen two golden ages: from the 1920s to the 1930s, and from the 1980s to the 1990s. The first heyday, starting in the New Culture Movement, demonstrated strong opposition to imperialism and feudalism. Progressive writers, exemplified by Lu Xun, pioneered China's modern literature; Lu Xun, Shen Congwen, Ba Jin, Mao Dun, Lao She and (Eileen) Zhang Ailing have since come to be regarded as great masters of Chinese literature.

The emergence in the 1980s and 1990s of a number of more internationally influenced writers and works reflects the achievements and richness of China's late-20th-century literature. Writers showed greater maturity in the use of contemporary language to express the lives and aesthetic experiences of modern Chinese people. Generally speaking, the artistry of thought and literary expression achieved by contemporary novelists surpassed that of the previous generation.

China has dozens of literary awards, the most prestigious of which are the Mao Dun Literary Award, the Lu Xun Literary Award, and the annual Zhonghua Literary Figure of the Year. Chinese Women's Literary Awards, held every five years, is a major national award scheme covering works by women in the fields of novels, prose, poetry, documentary writing, women's literary theory, and translation.

Internet Literature

Like elsewhere, China has seen the rapid emergence and flourishing of internet literary writing. Since the setting up in 1995 of "Olive Tree," the first Chinese literary website, a score or more of similar sites have sprung up. As a new literary medium, the emerging internet has to a certain degree changed the overall makeup of Chinese literature. China has also seen the mushrooming of blogs since 2006, with nearly 28 million users, many of whom are entertainment stars and cultural celebrities.

Opera

Chinese traditional opera, Greek drama and Indian Sanskrit opera are considered as the world's three ancient opera forms. China alone boasts more than 300 types of local opera including Peking Opera, Kunqu Opera, Shaoxing Opera, Yu Opera, Guangdong Opera, Sichuan Opera, Qinqiang Opera etc. Among them, Peking Opera is the most popular and influential form. Chinese traditional opera mainly expresses stories through song and dance forms.

Sichuan Opera

Modern drama was introduced from abroad in the early 20th century and came of age in the 1930s. Beijing People's Art Theater, founded in 1952, represents the apex of Chinese theater. The Theater has staged nearly 100 dramas, among which *Teahouse* enjoys international prestige as a classical drama. Cao Yu has been deemed as China's best dramatist.

The Plum Blossom Award is China's highest prize for young and middle-aged opera performers. To date, the prestigious award has gone to 551 actors and actresses in 47 types of opera.

A Peking Opera performance

Peking Opera

Peking Opera is regarded as the national opera. Over the last 200 years, Peking Opera has developed a repertoire of more than 1,000 plays, as well as sets of musical genres and stylized performance movements. Famous Peking Opera artists, including Mei Lanfang, Cheng Yanqiu, Ma Lianliang and Zhou Xinfang, emerged in the last century, and new artists continue to emerge in the 21st century.

Pipa, the Chinese lute

Erhu, a two-stringed
Chinese fiddle

Bamboo flute

Guqin, an ancient
Chinese harp

Quyi (folk art forms: rich in local flavor, e.g., ballad singing, storytelling, comic dialogues, clapper recitals)

Quyi is the name for traditional Chinese spoken and singing arts, and is a unique form of art developed over a long history from folk oral literature and song. At present, there are about 400 *Quyi* genres, including comic dialogues, Beijing musical storytelling with drum accompaniment, Yangzhou ditties, Shandong musical storytelling with drum, Anhui musical storytelling, song-and-dance duets in Northeast China, and Fengyang flower-drum. Comic dialogues and storytelling are the most widespread genres, commonly seen on TV and the stage.

Music

Dating as far back as the first century BC, there were over 80 Chinese musical instruments. In history, there were several flourishing periods for music culture. *Guangling Melody* and *Eighteen Stanzas for the Barbarian Reed Pipe* played on the *guqin*, *Ambush from All Sides* on the *pipa*, and *Spring Flowers on a Moonlit Night on the River* on Chinese wind or stringed instruments are representative of such ancient musical works.

Since the middle of the 20th century, along with the introduction of Western music and musical instruments, Chinese music has made historical developments. Musicians have created a number of outstanding works with national characteristics, including: *The East Is Red*, a large-scale music and dance epic; *The Red Guards on Honghu Lake*, an opera; and *The Yellow River Concerto*, for piano. Meanwhile, Chinese musicians and art performance troupes have participated in a variety of international exchanges and competitions, with many of them making remarkable achievements.

Large-scale music festivals are held regularly, for example, the annual Shanghai International Art Festival, Beijing International Music Festival and Beijing International Opera Season. They have attracted a great number of world-famous musicians and top-level music and art troupes to China.

Night Revels of Han Xizai (detail), painted in the Five Dynasties (907-960)

Dance

Chinese folk dancing has a long history, with the country's 56 ethnic groups creating many dances with unique characteristics, such as northern Han people's *yangge*, south China's tea-picking lantern dance, the Mongolian *andai* dance and the Tibetan *xuanzi* dance. In 1959, the National Ballet of China was founded, introducing Western ballet to China. To date, certain ballets, with their Chinese characteristics, such as *The Red Detachment of Women*, *The White-Haired Girl* and *Raise the Red Lantern*, have enjoyed wide popularity among people. During festivals, folk dancing is a popular form of entertainment; while national song and dance troupes, such as China Opera and Ballet Theater, China Oriental Song and Dance Troupe, Central Nationalities Song and Dance Ensemble and the National Ballet of China provide professional, high-standard performances to the people.

Yangge dance

Mongolian dance

Tibetan dance

Uyghur dance

Jade carving

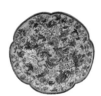
Cloisonné enamel

Clay figurines

Paper-cut

Lacquer work

Folk Arts and Crafts

China boasts a wide variety of arts and crafts renowned for excellent workmanship. In terms of technique, Chinese folk arts are categorized into cutting, bundling, plaiting, knitting, embroidering, carving, molding, and painting. They have strong local flavor and diverse folk styles. Special arts and crafts involve the use of precious or special materials, combined with elaborate designs and processes to produce works of great elegance. For example, jade carving uses jadestone raw material; Jingtai cloisonné enamel gets its name from the Jingtai reign of the Ming Dynasty (1450-1457), from blue glaze on copper filament, which after polishing reveals magnificence in design and color.

Fan painting

Painting on porcelain

Calligraphy and Painting

Chinese written characters are square-shaped, with an emphasis on vigor of style and structure. The art of calligraphy developed naturally from China's unique writing system. Every dynasty had its great calligraphers whose styles came to represent their times, and the Chinese people's love of calligraphy stems from that tradition.

Eastern Jin Dynasty calligraphy master Wang Xizhi's (321-379) renowned work *Preface to the Orchid Pavilion Poem Collection*

Different from Western oil painting, traditional Chinese painting is characterized by unique forms of expression. Its roots can be traced back to paintings on Neolithic pottery 6,000 to 7,000 years ago. Since similar tools were used to draw lines for the earliest painting and writing, painting and calligraphy were said to share the same origin. Chinese paintings often include poetry or calligraphy, and also have name seals stamped on the works; thus the four art forms are integrated, providing a richer aesthetic experience. Figure, landscape, and flower-and-bird paintings are major traditional painting genres, with masterpieces of different genres in different dynasties.

Contemporary painting and calligraphy are still flourishing. The National Art Museum of China and others hold individual or joint exhibitions every year, and many exhibitions of traditional Chinese painting have been held overseas. Chinese artists have also made remarkable progress in Western-style oil painting, woodcut and watercolor; and many have created works that combine traditional Chinese and Western techniques, adding brilliance to both forms. With various kinds of modern materials, forms, frameworks and genres, modern artworks have also played a role. New media artworks, including video, digital, animated and audio art, are now commonly seen at domestic and overseas exhibitions.

Riverside Scene During Qingming Festival (detail), created by Zhang Zeduan (12th century), a famous painter in the Northern Song Dynasty (960-1127), 528 cm in length and 24.8cm in height

Cinema

Realism has remained the mainstream of Chinese cinema. In the wave of film-making that rose in the mid-1980s, realistic works reached high levels of creativity in varied subject matters, styles and forms, and in the exploration and innovation of cinematic language. The "fifth-generation" directors, including Zhang Yimou, Chen Kaige and Huang Jianxin, rose to fame during this period, becoming international cinema celebrities. The late 1990s saw the emergence of a "sixth-generation" wave of directors, including Jia Zhangke, Wang Xiaoshuai, Zhang Yuan and Lou Ye, who were mostly born in the 1960s and 1970s. Their movies portray ordinary people's lives in a realistic fashion.

Curse of the Golden Flower

In 2007, more than 400 domestic movies were made with the box office figure of 3.3 billion yuan, about 60% of total revenues. *Assembly*, a film made by director Feng Xiaogang who has continuously made box office records, and *The Warlords*, a film made by director Chen Kexin, each earned more than 200 million yuan. Furthermore, many domestic movies with box office totals of more than 30 million yuan have become the mainstay of cinemas.

Assembly

The Changchun and Shanghai international film festivals are annual events. The "Golden Rooster" is the top prize for Chinese movies. The government has specially established the "Ornamental Pillar" award to encourage the development of mainstream movies. The "Hundred Flowers Prize" is awarded on the basis of audience votes.

Cultural Exchanges

"Culture weeks," "culture tours," "culture festivals," "cultural years" and other events hosted jointly by China and overseas counterparts in recent years have deepened contact and understanding between diverse peoples, and offered new channels for equal dialogue between different civilizations. So far, China has reached government cultural agreements with 143 countries and signed 700 plans for annual cultural exchanges. Every year the Ministry of Culture authorizes 2,000 cultural exchange programs with 60 to 70 countries, involving some 30,000 participants.

The opera *Farewell My Concubine*, presented at the Lincoln Center, New York, January 2008, by the National Opera of China

Mass Media

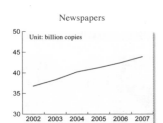

Newspapers

Unit: billion copies

50
45
40
35
30
2002 2003 2004 2005 2006 2007

Newspapers

Presently, the number of daily newspapers published in China exceeds 1,000, with their circulation reaching 100 million people, the highest of any country. Targeted at different reader groups, the newspapers are becoming more diversified.

Recent years have seen a trend of reorganization of newspapers. To date, nearly 40 newspaper groups have been established, including the Beijing Daily Group, Wenhui-Xinmin United Press Group, and Guangzhou Daily Press Group. In 2006, the Tianjin Daily News Group adopted digital technology in its distribution and, via satellite transmission, began serving immediate-printing and real-time reading of its *Tianjin Daily* in 39 countries.

Equipment room in CCTV

Radio

China National Radio, China's official radio station, has nine channels broadcasting over 200 hours per day via satellite. Every province, autonomous region and municipality also has its own radio stations.

China Radio International (CRI) is the only state radio station targeting overseas audience. It has 1,000 hours of programs beamed daily across the globe, in 38 foreign languages, in addition to standard Chinese (*putonghua*) and four Chinese dialects.

Television

China's television industry has a complete system with high-tech program production, transmission and coverage. China Central Television (CCTV), the state station, has 17 channels that broadcast over 360 hours of programs each day. Every province, autonomous region and municipality has its own TV station. Large international expositions, including the Shanghai TV Festival, Beijing International TV Week, China Radio and TV Expo, and Sichuan TV Festival, are held on a regular basis. Besides judging and conferring awards, these festivals conduct academic exchanges and import and export of TV programs.

Hours of Broadcasts and TV Programs

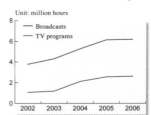

TV series produced

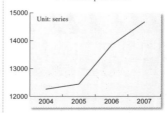

Coverage rate of broadcasts and TV programs

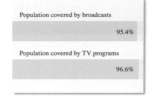

Watching a TV program on a mobile phone.

Website of http://www.china.org.cn

Internet and Multimedia

Since the mid-1990s, China's traditional media has joined hands with online media and, of its over 10,000 news media, 2,000 have gone online. Popular news websites have mushroomed to play a unique role in news reports.

Online magazines have developed rapidly, with the total circulation exceeding 360 million. After China Mobile launched cell-phone TV service in 2005, news images and text have been available on mobile phones, prompting a spate of new websites to also provide cell-phone reports. In August 2006, the General Administration of Press and Publication launched a project to explore forms of digital publication and the operating modes of online, cell-phone and electronic newspapers.

The newest trend in China's media industry is to form intermedia and transregional media operating on multiple patterns. In 2001, the government set a goal of establishing transregional multimedia news groups, and instituted detailed regulations on fund-raising, foreign cooperation and trans-media expansion. The China Radio, Film and TV Group, founded in late 2001, is now China's largest and most powerful multi-media group, covering television, internet, publishing, advertising, etc., thanks to integrating the resources of national radio, TV and film organizations, along with those of internet firms. CCTV's English channel reaches US audience via News Group's Fox News network.

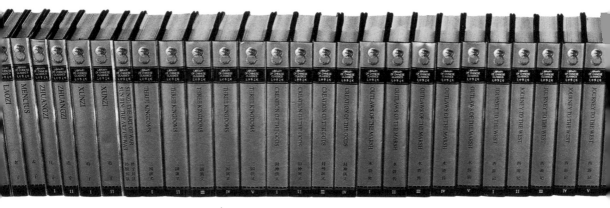

Library of Chinese Classics, a large-scale publishing project

Publishing

China produces the most publications in the world, with over six billion copies of books and about three billion copies of magazines put out annually. In line with China's WTO commitments, the General Administration of Press and Publication in May 2003 promulgated its Administrative Measures on Foreign-invested Book, Newspaper and Periodical Distribution Enterprises, allowing foreign investors to engage in publication retailing as of May 1, 2003, and wholesaling from December 1, 2004; but the Administration's approval is required for any such retail or wholesale organization to be opened. So far, some 60 foreign-funded enterprises have set up agencies in China's mainland, in preparation to apply or applying to form such distributors.

Books

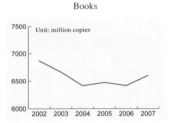

Periodicals

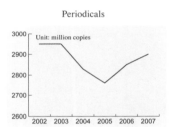

Featured Topics

Events in 2007
30 Events During 30 Years of Reform
  and Opening-up
Beijing 2008 Olympic Games
Massive Quake in Wenchuan, Sichuan

Events in 2007

In 2007, China's GDP grew by 11.9%; total grain output exceeded 500 billion kg again, guaranteeing price control and market stability; fiscal revenue exceeded 5,000 billion yuan, an increase of over 30% compared with 2006; personal incomes increased by a large margin, with urban income increasing by nearly 10%, while rural per-capita net income rose by over 12%; and employment figures in urban areas grew by 12,040,000, the highest growth in recent years.

By the end of December 2007, the number of netizens in China had reached 210 million, 73 million more than in 2006.

Starting from January, a total of 150 million rural students in China were exempted from paying tuition and incidental fees for their nine-year compulsory education.

On March 16, the Property Law of the PRC and the Enterprise Income Tax Law of the PRC were adopted at the Fifth Session of the 10th National People's Congress (NPC). Coming into effect as of October 1, 2007, the Property Law expressly specifies that the state equally protects public as well as private property. The Enterprise Income Tax Law integrates the taxation systems for domestic and foreign enterprises, as of January 1, 2008. On March 22, the China Banking Regulatory Commission released its "Report on Opening up China's Banking Industry to Foreign Investment," expressly encouraging the establishment of foreign-funded banks with legal status, clearly stating that foreign banks are encouraged to set up branches in China.

At the end of May, cyanobacterial contamination broke out in the Taihu Lake, Wuxi, resulting in a drinking-water crisis for nearly 1,000,000 people. Later, similar outbreaks occurred in the Dianchi and then Chaohu lakes. As an ecological warning against negative effects brought by high economic growth rates, the "Taihu Lake Incident" became a benchmark for eastern China and the whole country, urging accelerated transformation of the growth mode and establishment of the "Scientific Outlook on Development."

On June 4, China's National Climate Change Program was formally launched, comprehensively elucidating national measures for tackling the issue of climate change before 2010. It was the first policy-related document of China on the issue of climate change, as well as the first related national program of developing countries.

On June 29, the Labor Contract Law of the PRC was adopted at the Standing Committee of the 10th NPC, for the purposes of improving the labor contractual system, clarifying the rights and obligations of both parties in labor contracts, and protecting the legitimate rights and interests of employees. The law will come into force as of January 1, 2008.

On July 11, the State Council issued a notice on setting up a subsistence allowance system for rural residents, in order to practically solve the livelihood problems of impoverished rural people, China's lowest-income group. Altogether 3 billion yuan was appropriated by the state treasury for rural subsistence allowances, and more than 20 million impoverished rural residents were covered by this system.

On September 13, the National Bureau of Corruption Prevention was established.

In September, the National Grand Theater was completed in Beijing. As a large world-class theater for the arts, it was French-designed and Chinese-built.

Incomplete statistics show that in October 2007, there were about 130 million accounts and more than 5,000 institutional investors in the Shanghai and Shenzhen stock markets; while the securitization ratio, as an important index of the development level of a country's securities market, had reached 100 percent.

From October 15 to 21, the 17th National Congress of the Communist Party of China (CPC) was held in Beijing, of vital importance and at a crucial stage of China's reform and development. The Congress defined the goal, approach and theoretical system for China's future development, and also included the "Scientific Outlook on Development" in the CPC Constitution.

On October 24, China's first lunar probe, Chang'e-1 was successfully launched at the Xichang Satellite Launch Center. On November 26, from its lunar orbit 380,000 km away from the Earth, Chang'e-1 sent back the first pictures of the moon's surface, marking the success of first lunar exploration by China, becoming one of the few countries in the world with deep-space exploration capacity.

On December 29, "The Decision on Methods for Selecting the Chief Executive and Forming the Legislative Council of Hong Kong SAR in 2012 and Issues on Universal Suffrage" was adopted at the 31st Session of the Standing Committee of the 10th NPC. Accordingly, appropriate amendments may be made to specific methods for selecting the fourth-term Chief Executive and for forming the fifth-term Legislative Council of the HKSAR in 2012; the election of the fifth-term Chief Executive of the HKSAR in 2017 may be implemented by the method of universal suffrage; after which the election of the HKSAR Legislative Council may be implemented by electing all members by universal suffrage.

30 Events During 30 Years of Reform and Opening-up

In 1978, the policy of reform and opening-up was decided at the Third Plenary Session of the 11th Central Committee of the Communist Party of China (CPCCC).

From December 18 to 22, the Third Plenary Session of the 11th CPCCC was held, at which the new policy of reform and opening-up was adopted, marking the historic point when China started to shift its central task to economic development.

In 1979, special economic zones were established.

On August 13, the State Council issued its Provisions on Some Issues Concerning Foreign Trade Development to Increase Foreign Exchange Revenue, which proposed to expand the foreign-trade authority of local governments and enterprises, and encouraged the establishment of more export and export-oriented special zones. On May 16, 1980, the CPCCC and the State Council formally renamed "special zones" as "economic special zones."

In 1982, the rural household responsibility system with remuneration linked to output was established.

In 1978, economic restructuring was first launched in rural China. Its major measure was to spread the household responsibility system with remuneration linked to output. On January 1, 1982, the CPCCC approved and promoted the "Outlines of the National Rural Work Conference," affirming the system.

In 1984, a planned commodity economy was proposed.

On October 20, the Third Plenary Session of the 12th CPCCC was held, at which "The Decision of the CPCCC on Economic System Reform" was adopted. The Decision stated that "the socialist planned economy is a planned commodity economy based on public ownership."

In 1986, the reform of enterprises owned by the entire people was launched.

On December 5, the State Council issued its Provisions on Deepening Reform of Enterprises and Enhancing Their Vitality, which proposed that small enterprises owned by all the people could be operated in the form of leasing or contracting on a trial basis, while large and medium-sized enterprises should adopt the responsibility system for operation in various forms. Each region could choose a few large and medium-sized people-owned enterprises with developed conditions to experiment the shareholding system.

In 1987, the basic line of "one central task and two focal points" was put forward.

From October 25 to November 1, the 13th CPC National Congress was held. The Congress put forward the Party's basic line of "one central task and two focal points" in the primary stage of socialism: taking economic development as the central task, while adhering to the "Four Cardinal Principles" and persevering in reform and opening-up.

In 1988, "science and technology as the primary productive forces" was put forward.

On March 13, 1985, the CPCCC issued "The Decision on the Reform of the Science and Technology Management System," which pointed out that "modern science and technology are the most active and decisive factors among new social productive forces." On September 5, 1988, Deng Xiaoping brought forth the famed conclusion: "Science and technology are the primary productive forces."

In 1992, the goal for socialist market economic reform was set.

From October 12 to 18, the 14th CPC National Congress was held. The Congress summarized practical experience since the Third Plenary Session of the 11th CPCCC, and set the goal for national economic restructuring: to establish a socialist market economy.

In 1993, it was proposed to build a modern corporate system.

From November 11 to 14, the Third Plenary Session of the 14th CPCCC was held. The Session adopted "The CPCCC Decision on Some Issues Concerning the Establishment of the Socialist Market Economy," which pointed out: "To establish the socialist market economy is to set up a modern corporate system characterized by clearly established ownership, well-defined power and responsibility, separation of enterprise management from government administration, and scientific management adapted to the market economy."

In 1993, reform of the tax distribution system was launched.

On December 15, the State Council issued its "Decision on Implementing the Tax Distribution System for the Financial Management System." This entailed institutional reform of the governmental financial system, covering the widest scope and making the largest adjustments with the deepest influence since the founding of New China in 1949.

In 1993, the goals of financial system reform were set.

On December 25, the State Council issued its "Decision on Reform of the Financial System," which set the goals for financial system reform: to set up a macro-regulatory system with the People's Bank of China as the central bank that independently implements monetary policy under the leadership of the State Council; to set up a financial organization system that separates policy finance from commercial finance, with state-commercial banks as the core and different financial institutions coexisting; and to build a financial market system that is uniform and open, with orderly competition and strict administration.

In 1994, comprehensive and coordinated reform of the foreign-trade regime was launched.

On January 11, the State Council issued its "Decision on Deepening Reform of the Foreign Trade Regime," putting forward the goals for reform: unified policies, open operation, fair competition, sole responsibility for own profits and losses, integration of industry and foreign trade, an agency system, and establishment of operation mechanisms consistent with prevailing international rules.

In 1994, housing reform was launched.

On July 18, the State Council issued its "Decision on Deepening Reform of the Urban Housing System," specifying the contents of reform, including turning the welfare-oriented public housing allocation system into a housing distribution system based on income, which follows the practice of "distribution according to work", and setting up a housing provident fund system. The issuance of the Decision pushed forward the marketization of housing.

In 1995, the goal of "two fundamental changes" was proposed.

From September 25 to 28, the Fifth Plenary Session of the 14th CPCCC was held. The Session approved the Proposal of the CPCCC on "Promulgating the Ninth Five-Year Plan for National Economic and Social Development and Long-range Goals for 2010," which proposed two fundamental changes with overall significance for China: one, to transform the economic system from the traditional planned one to a socialist market economy; the other, to change the mode of economic growth from extensive to intensive.

In 1996, major progress was made in the reform of the foreign-exchange management system.

On December 1, China accepted the obligations of Article VIII of the "Agreement of Articles" of the International Monetary Fund and realized full convertibility of RMB under current accounts, marking major progress in the reform of China's foreign-exchange management system.

In 1997, the basic program for the primary stage of socialism was put forward.

From September 12 to 18, the 15th National Congress of the CPC was held, at which the basic program for the primary stage of socialism was put forward: building a socialist economy with Chinese characteristics means developing a market economy under socialism and constantly emancipating and developing the productive forces; building socialist politics with Chinese characteristics means ruling the country by law and developing socialist democracy under the leadership of the CPC and with the people as the masters of the country; building a socialist culture with Chinese characteristics means taking Marxism as guidance, aiming to train citizens in high ideals, moral integrity, good education and strong sense of discipline, and developing a national, scientific and popular socialist culture geared to the needs of modernization, the world and the future.

In 1999, it was clarified that the non-public sectors of the economy constitute an important component of the socialist market economy.

From March 5 to 15, the Second Session of the Ninth NPC was held, adopting Amendments to the Constitution of the PRC, clarifying for the first time that non-public sectors of the economy constitute an important component of the socialist market economy.

In 1999, the Western Development Strategy was proposed.

On March 22, the State Council issued its "Recommendations on Furthering the Development of Western China," putting forward 10 recommendations for promoting and launching western regional development.

In 2001, China was formally admitted into the World Trade Organization (WTO).

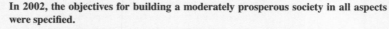

On November 10, the WTO's Fourth Ministerial Conference, in Doha, Qatar, adopted documents for the accession of China; and China became a new WTO member.

In 2002, the objectives for building a moderately prosperous society in all aspects were specified.

From November 8 to 14, the 16th National Congress of the CPC was held, putting forward the objectives for building a moderately prosperous society in all aspects: building a moderately prosperous society of a higher standard in the first decade of the 21st century; and turning China into a strong, prosperous, democratic and culturally advanced modern socialist country by mid-century.

In 2003, the strategy for revitalizing Northeast China and other old industrial bases was put forward.

On September 10, the State Council's regular meeting adopted the guiding concept, principles, tasks, policies and measures for revitalizing Northeast China and other old industrial bases. On September 29, General Secretary Hu Jintao presided over a politburo meeting of the CPCCC, which pointed out: the important strategic task of revitalizing Northeast China and other old industrial bases.

In 2004, it was proposed to develop capital markets.

On January 31, the State Council issued its "Opinions on Promoting Reform, Opening-up and Steady Growth of Capital Markets," making it clear that China would work hard to develop capital markets.

In 2004, the shareholding system reform of state-owned commercial banks was launched.

The Bank of China Co. Ltd. was established on August 26, while China Construction Bank Co. Ltd. was set up on September 21, 2004. The two wholly state-owned commercial banks were restructured into state-controlled commercial banks.

In 2004, the Constitution included an article stating, "the lawful private property of citizens may not be encroached upon."

On March 14, the Second Session of the 10th NPC deliberated on and adopted the fourth Amendments to the Constitution of the PRC, including "the lawful private property of citizens may not be encroached upon" and "the state respects and protects human rights."

In 2005, the pilot untradable share reform of listed companies was launched.

Approved by the State Council, on April 29, the China Securities Regulatory Commission issued the "Notice on Pilot Untradable Share Reform of Listed Companies," announcing the launch of the pilot untradable share reform of listed companies. One year later, major progress or interim achievements were made in Chinese capital markets in five aspects: untradable share reform, increased standards of listed companies, comprehensive control of securities companies, expanding of institutional investors, and improvement of market laws.

In 2005, the important historic task of building a new socialist countryside was proposed.

On October 11, the Fifth Plenary Session of the 16th CPCCC adopted the "Recommendations of the CPCCC on Drafting the 11th Five-Year Plan for National Economic and Social Development," defining the goals and action programs for China's economic and social development in the next five years, and putting forward the important historic task of building a new socialist countryside.

In 2006, Regulations of the PRC on Agricultural Taxation was abrogated.

On December 29, 2005, the 19th meeting of the Standing Committee of the 10th NPC adopted its "Decision on Abolishing the Regulations of the PRC on Agricultural Taxation." From January 1, 2006, the Chinese government abolished agricultural, special agricultural products and livestock taxes.

In 2006, the building of a harmonious socialist society was proposed.

From October 8 to 11, the Sixth Plenary Session of the 16th CPCCC was held, approving the "Decision of the CPCCC on Several Important Issues Concerning the Building of a Harmonious Socialist Society," specifying that "increasing the capacity for building a harmonious socialist society" is an important part of the Party's governance capacity.

In 2007, the Property Law was promulgated.

On March 16, the Fifth Session of the 10th NPC adopted the Property Law of the PRC, which came into effect as of October 1, 2007. The Law specifies that the state protects public as well as private property.

In 2007, the "Scientific Outlook on Development" was included in the CPC Constitution.

From October 15 to 21, the 17th National Congress of the CPC was held. At the Session, the "Scientific Outlook on Development" was included in the Constitution of the Party, a great historic contribution of the 17th National Congress.

The Emblem of the Beijing 2008 Olympic Games

同一个世界　同一个梦想
One World One Dream

 ## Beijing 2008 Olympic Games

In 1979, China resumed its legitimate seat in the United Nations. In 1981, He Zhen-liang was elected as member of the International Olympic Committee (IOC), marking a new historical period in the relationship between China and Olympic sports, and coope-ration between China and the IOC. In 1984, China sent a delegation to the Los Angeles Olympic Games. From then on, the Chinese people have been appreciating the honors and joys of the Olympics.

In July 2001, Beijing won the bid to host the 2008 Olympic Games. The Beijing Organizing Committee for the Games of the XXIX Olympiad (BOCOG), founded in the same year, determined the concepts for the 2008 Games: "Green Olympics, High-tech Olympics, and People's Olympics."

"Green Olympics" refers to organizing the Olympics based on concepts of protecting the environment, energy and resources and ecological balance. "High-tech Olympics" refers to making full use of scientific and technological innovations nationwide, to hold a grand sporting event with a high degree of science and technology. "People's Olympics" refers to delivering ideas for a modern Olympics, advancing cultural exchange between China and the world, deepening the friendship and mutual understanding of peoples from different countries, and satisfying all participants through constant effort, by providing the best possible natural and social environments.

Emblem: Chinese Seal – Dancing Beijing

Slogan: "One World, One Dream"

Mascots: Fuwa – Beibei, Jingjing, Huanhuan, Yingying, and Nini ("Bei-Jing Huan-Ying Ni" means "Beijing welcomes you")

Opening time: 8:08 pm on August 8, 2008

Date: August 6-24, 2008

Sports: 28 sports, containing 302 events. There will be 47 gold medals for athletics events, the sports category with the most gold medals in the Beijing Olympic Games. Football matches will be held before the opening ceremony.

In the Beijing 2008 Olympic Games, people will have the chance to appreciate the amazing Beijing 2008 Wushu Tournament, staged from August 21 to 24, 2008. The Tournament will offer 10 gold medals, 8 for the routine competition (Men's Changquan Boxing, Nanquan Boxing, Broadsword and Cudgel; and Women's Changquan Boxing, Shadow Boxing, Spear and Rapier), and 2 for the Free Combat competition.

Fuwa, the mascots for the Beijing 2008 Olympic Games

The Torch for the Beijing 2008
Olympic Games

The Medals for the Beijing 2008 Olympic Games

Liu Changchun, the first Chinese athlete
participating in the Olympics in 1932

Yao Ming, Chinese basketball star

The Olympic Spirit in China

The Olympic spirit is firstly a spirit of participation, participation being more important than victory. In 1932, Chinese athlete Liu Changchun went to Los Angeles on his own, after traveling for 21 days on the sea, and competed in the 100-meter race of the 10th Olympic Games, the first time that a Chinese participated in the Olympics. Although the fatigued Liu ultimately failed to win, he did demonstrate Chinese people's spirit of participation to the world.

The Olympic spirit is a "Swifter, Higher and Stronger" spirit. Since 1949, China has sent delegations to six summer Olympics and eight winter Olympics. In terms of total Olympic gold, China ranked fourth in the Los Angeles, Barcelona and Atlanta Olympics, and second in the Athens Games.

The Olympic spirit is also a spirit of universality and unity. Beijing is working hard to host a better Olympics for the world. The 1.3 billion Chinese people will, together with athletes from all over the world, enjoy this year's grand Games, enhancing unity and friendship.

The Olympic Flame was lit at Olympia, Greece, March 24, 2008.

The sacred flame of the Beijing 2008 Olympic Games successfully ascended Qomolangma, the world's highest summit, May 8, 2008.

Beijing 2008 Paralympics

The 13th Paralympics will be held in Beijing from September 6 to 17, 2008. There are 20 venues, among which 16 are in Beijing, for 18 sports. For accessibility, most of the venues are in the Olympic Green or at universities. Sailing and equestrian events will be held in the Qingdao venue and Hong Kong venue, respectively.

The 2008 Paralympic Games cover 20 sports: archery, athletics, boccia, cycling, equestrian, football 5-a-side, football 7-a-side, goalball, judo, powerlifting, rowing, sailing, shooting, swimming, table tennis, volleyball sitting, wheelchair basketball, wheelchair fencing, wheelchair rugby, and wheelchair tennis. According to the rules of the Paralympics, all the sports are graded according to the type and degree of disability; altogether, 471 gold medals are offered. Over 4,000 athletes and over 2,500 coaches and officials from 150 countries and regions will participate in the Paralympics.

The Emblem of the Beijing 2008 Paralympic Games

"Bird's Nest," the main venue for the Beijing 2008 Olympic Games

The Emblem of the Shanghai
Special Olympics

Shanghai 2007 Special Olympics World Summer Games

From October 2 to 11, 2007, Shanghai hosted the 12th Special Olympics World Summer Games. These grand Games involved over 7,400 athletes and coaches, along with more than 20,000 parents, experts, invited personages and volunteers from over 160 countries and regions.

The Special Olympics include 21 competitions (athletics, balls, powerlifting, gymnastics, judo, sailing, equestrian, kayaking, etc.) and 4 non-sports events.

The theme of the Special Olympics is, "I know I can." The theme expresses the spirit of the Special Olympics athletes striving unceasingly for self-improvement. The essence of the Special Olympics is reflected in: "Equality and Tolerance." This also embodies the concept and mission of the Special Olympics – "participate, share joy, exchange skills and promote friendship."

The Chinese delegation participated in all the competitions as well as non-sports events, and won 463 gold medals, 336 silver medals and 258 bronze medals.

Volunteers for the Beijing Olympics
receiving English language training

Volunteers

Over 70,000 volunteers would be needed for the Olympic Games, and another 30,000 for the Paralympic Games. The majority of volunteers of the Olympic and Paralympic Games will be recruited from universities in Beijing. BOCOG also plans to recruit a certain number of volunteers from residents nationwide, as well as compatriots from Taiwan, Hong Kong and Macao, overseas Chinese, students studying abroad, and foreigners.

The volunteer recruitment started from August 2006 and will end by March 2008. By January 2008, the number of applicants exceeded 800,000, and 80,000 have been initially selected. The BOCOG Volunteer Department and other organizations have conducted general training for selected volunteers. Professional volunteers have finished professional training courses; while volunteers for sports events have participated in training at the venues and at-the-post training. Teacher training for the Paralympics volunteers has started.

Olympic Medals and Winners

In 1984 at the Los Angeles Olympic Games, Chinese athlete Xu Haifeng won the gold medal in 50m pistol, the first gold for China in its Olympic history. From then on, Chinese athletes altogether won 112 gold medals at summer Olympics. In 2004 at the Athens Olympic Games, Chinese athletes won 32 gold medals, including 10 athletes below the age of 20. At the last Olympics, competitors from China made great achievements in athletics, kayaking, and table tennis. Liu Xiang won the gold medal in the men's 110-meter hurdles, in 12.91 seconds, equaling the world record and creating a new Olympic record, as well as giving China its first Olympic gold in men's track and field. Meng Guanliang and Yang Wenjun won the gold medal in men's C-2 500 meters, a first for China in aquatic sports. Sun Tiantian and Sun Ting won China's first Olympic tennis gold in women's doubles tennis.

Table tennis, badminton, gymnastics and diving were among the sports in which Chinese athletes won the most gold medals in previous summer Olympics. Chinese athletes also won gold medals in swimming, shooting, weightlifting, fencing, middle-distance race, race walk, judo, and wrestling.

Xu Haifeng, the first Chinese athlete to win an Olympic gold medal, in 1984

Total Number of Medals Won by China's Olympic Delegation

Year/Session	🥇	🥈	🥉	Total	Rank
1984/ 23rd Los Angeles Games	15	8	9	32	4th
1988/ 24th Seoul Games	5	11	12	28	11th
1992/ 25th Barcelona Games	16	22	16	54	4th
1996/ 26th Atlanta Games	16	22	12	50	4th
2000/ 27th Sydney Games	28	16	15	59	3rd
2004/ 28th Athens Games	32	17	14	63	2nd

Liu Xiang, world champion in men's 110m hurdle

 Paralympics Medals and Winners

In 1984, China sent its first delegation to the Seventh Paralympic Games held in New York, the United States. Subsequently, China participated in five Paralympics in succession, for which it altogether sent 215 athletes, and won 80 gold medals; 59 athletes broke 75 world records, and 25 broke Paralympic records. In 2004 at the 12th Paralympic Games, the 200 disabled Chinese athletes won 63 gold medals in 284 events, classified under 11 sports, ranking first among the 136 competing countries and regions.

He Junquan, winner of four Paralympic gold medals in swimming

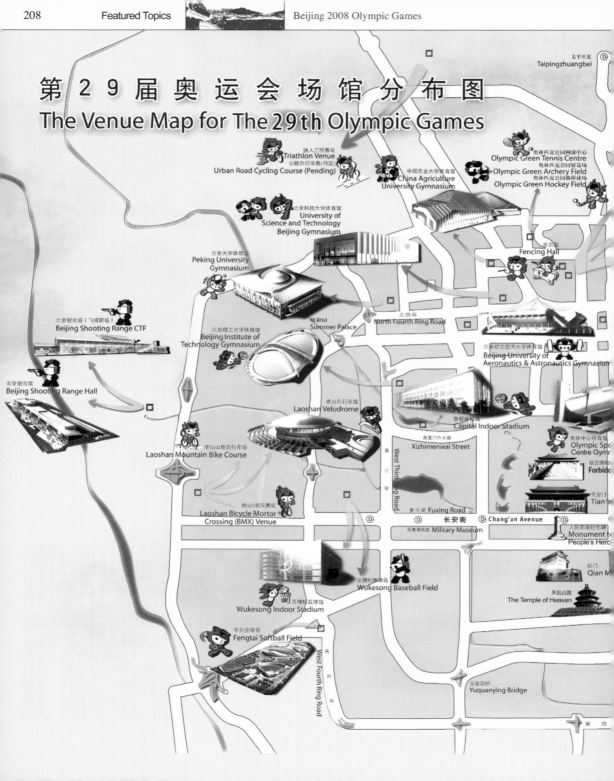

第２９届奥运会场馆分布图
The Venue Map for The 29th Olympic Games

太平庄北
Taipingzhuangbei

铁人三项赛场
Triathlon Venue
公路自行车赛(特定)
Urban Road Cycling Course (Pending)

中国农业大学体育馆
China Agriculture
University Gymnasium

奥林匹克公园网球中心
Olympic Green Tennis Centre
奥林匹克公园射箭场
Olympic Green Archery Field
奥林匹克公园曲棍球场
Olympic Green Hockey Field

北京科技大学体育馆
University of
Science and Technology
Beijing Gymnasium

击剑馆
Fencing Hall

北京大学体育馆
Peking University
Gymnasium

北四环
North Fourth Ring Road

北京射击场(飞碟靶场)
Beijing Shooting Range CTF

北京理工大学体育馆
Beijing Institute of
Technology Gymnasium

颐和园
Summer Palace

北京航空航天大学体育馆
Beijing University of
Aeronautics & Astronautics Gymnasium

北京射击馆
Beijing Shooting Range Hall

老山自行车馆
Laoshan Velodrome

首都体育馆
Capital Indoor Stadium

西直门外大街
Xizhimenwai Street

西三环路
West Third Ring Road

奥体中心体育场
Olympic Sp
Centre Gym

老山山地自行车场
Laoshan Mountain Bike Course

故宫博物
Forbid

复兴路 Fuxing Road

天安门
Tian'

老山小轮车赛场
Laoshan Bicycle Mortor
Crossing (BMX) Venue

长安街 Chang'an Avenue

人民英雄纪念碑
Monument t
People's Hero

军事博物馆 Military Museum

五棵松棒球场
Wukesong Baseball Field

前门
Qian M

五棵松篮球馆
Wukesong Indoor Stadium

天坛公园
The Temple of Heaven

丰台垒球场
Fengtai Softball Field

西四环路
West Fourth Ring Road

玉泉营桥
Yuquanying Bridge

南四

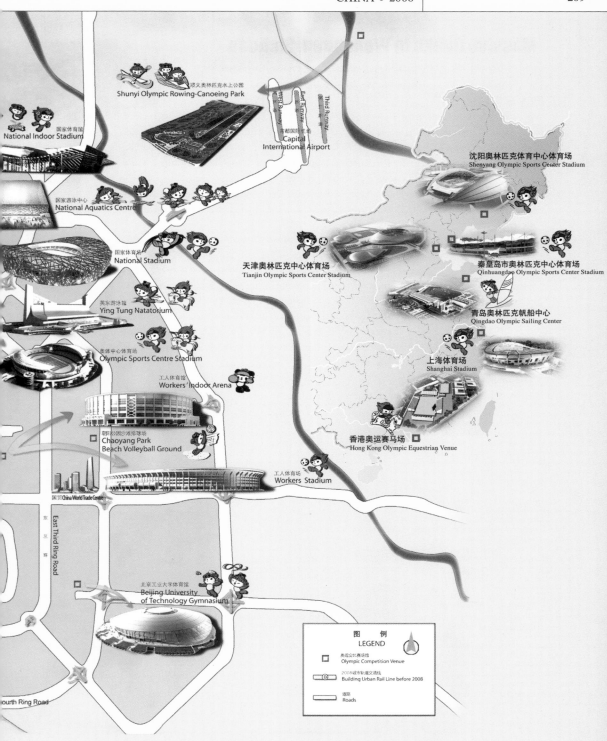

Shunyi Olympic Rowing-Canoeing Park
顺义奥林匹克水上公园

National Indoor Stadium
国家体育馆

East Runway
West Runway
Third Runway
首都国际机场
Capital International Airport

沈阳奥林匹克体育中心体育场
Shenyang Olympic Sports Center Stadium

国家游泳中心
National Aquatics Centre

国家体育场
National Stadium

天津奥林匹克中心体育场
Tianjin Olympic Sports Center Stadium

秦皇岛市奥林匹克中心体育场
Qinhuangdao Olympic Sports Center Stadium

英东游泳馆
Ying Tung Natatorium

青岛奥林匹克帆船中心
Qingdao Olympic Sailing Center

奥体中心体育场
Olympic Sports Centre Stadium

上海体育场
Shanghai Stadium

工人体育馆
Workers' Indoor Arena

朝阳公园沙滩排球场
Chaoyang Park Beach Volleyball Ground

国贸 China World Trade Centre

香港奥运赛马场
Hong Kong Olympic Equestrian Venue

工人体育场
Workers Stadium

东三环
East Third Ring Road

北京工业大学体育馆
Beijing University of Technology Gymnasium

Fourth Ring Road

图 例
LEGEND

奥运会比赛场馆
Olympic Competition Venue

2008年城市轨道交通线
Building Urban Rail Line before 2008

道路
Roads

Massive Quake in Wenchuan, Sichuan

History will forever remember the moment: 14:28 on May 12, 2008.

History will forever remember the place: Wenchuan County in southwest China's Sichuan Province.

Magnitude: 8.0; intensity: 11 degrees

Shortly after the earthquake, Hu Jintao, General Secretary of the CPC Central Committee, PRC President and Chairman of the CPC Central Military Commission, gave the national mobilization order for rescue and relief, immediately assembling PLA soldiers and armed police. He urged the swiftest possible rescue of victims and the safeguarding of people's security in stricken areas. Wen Jiabao, Premier of the State Council and commander-in-chief for the State Council general headquarters for disaster-relief work, flew directly to the quake-hit area to oversee the rescue work.

The massive Wenchuan earthquake became the country's worst disaster, with the most extensive scale of devastation, presenting the challenge of the most difficult relief work, since the founding of New China in 1949. When it occurred, tremors were felt in dozens of provinces, autonomous regions and centrally administered municipalities, including Beijing, Jiangsu, Guizhou, Ningxia, Qinghai, Gansu, Henan, Shanxi, Shaanxi, Shandong, Yunnan, Hunan, Hubei, Shanghai, Chongqing, and Tibet. Besides Sichuan, the provinces of Gansu, Shaanxi and Yunnan were affected by this massive disaster in varying degrees. As of 12:00 p.m. on June 1, 2008, the death toll reached 69,016, with the total injured at 368,545, 18,830 people missing, and a population of more than 45 million in affected areas.

Gansu

Beijing

Shanxi

Wenchuan

Shaanxi

Sichuan
Chongqing

Hubei

Guizhou

Yunnan

The old town of Beichuan County, Sichuan, devastated in the earthquake

Figures About the Wenchuan Earthquake

Deaths	69,016 persons
Injured	368,545 persons
Missing	18,830 persons
Population affected by the quake	45,552,900 persons
Collapsed houses	6,525,000 rooms
Damaged houses	23,143,000 rooms
Devastated national or provincial expressways	15
Damaged railways	5
Loss of livestock and poultry	44,335,600
Rescue-and-relief troops of PLA and Armed Police Force	130,000 persons
Rescue-and-relief policemen and firefighters	20,000 persons
Medical rescue personnel	91,300 persons
Professional rescue workers	5,257 persons
Volunteers	80,000 persons
Isolated survivors rescued	698,000 persons
Buried survivors rescued	6,541 persons
Injured receiving treatment	360,000 persons
People transferred to and settled in safe areas	15,147,400 persons
Funds allocated by governments at various levels	20.609 billion yuan
Nationwide donations	37.307 billion yuan
Donations from governments of various countries	75 million US dollars

(Data by 12pm, June 1, 2008)

Risking dangers of aftershocks, further collapses and landslides, rescue officers and soldiers saved many lives in Beichuan.

Land routes into the quake-hit areas were wrecked. Nearly 100 helicopters from the air force and civil aviation made several thousand flights to open an "air lifeline," carrying relief materials and transporting out the injured.

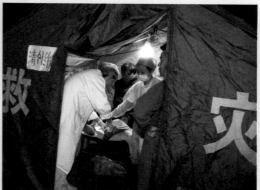

At the May 20 UN Security Council meeting, Ban Ki-moon and all present observed a minute of silence in tribute to the quake victims. Many countries' heads of state and government leaders visited Chinese embassies to extend their condolences to the victims and their sympathy, friendship and support to the Chinese people.

Late at night, medical rescuers still working at a makeshift clinic. As epidemic prevention work was launched timely, no epidemic diseases spread in the quake-hit areas.

After overall reconstruction was launched in the quake-hit areas, social order and people's daily lives were gradually restored.

"People's lives above all else," and "people's interests above all else." The country immediately activated an emergency plan for disaster relief. More than 150,000 PLA officers and personnel, armed police, public security police, along with local cadre and residents, as well as tens of thousands of rescuers and volunteers from all over the country, all braved hardship and danger to engage in the rescue work in those disaster-stricken areas. The firm leadership of the Central Authorities, along with the national spirit of resolutely uniting as one, was demonstrated everywhere in the work of relief, transfer and resettlement of affected people.

As of June 1, 2008, the Central Government and all levels of local government had already allocated almost 23 billion yuan and vast quantities of urgently needed goods to the disaster-stricken areas. There was also support from many other countries, as well as immeasurable quantities of nongovernmental donations from within and outside the country. People from various backgrounds, including compatriots in Hong Kong, Macao and Taiwan and overseas Chinese, all extended a helping hand to the disaster areas in a range of ways. In addition, Russia, Japan, South Korea and Singapore, etc., sent professional rescue and medical teams to help save many quake victims.

A nationwide three-minute silence, as tribute to the victims of the Wenchuan earthquake, was held at 14:28 on May 19. At that same moment, all around the country, horns of motor-vehicles, trains and ships wailed, along with air-raid sirens. The mourning expressed deep grief of the whole nation over the victims of the quake, as well as consolation to and encouragement for the survivors.

his is a "tent school" in Mian-hu Stadium, which became a uge temporary shelter.

People from all backgrounds across China have been doing their best to help those affected by the quake. This is a temporary blood-donation station in the Shanghai Exhibition Center set by the Shanghai Blood Center.

Extensive temporary housing settlements were built for those made homeless. The reconstruction program is being planned; reconstruction is to be completed in three years.

Appendix

Some Commonly Used Websites

Chinese Government

http://english.gov.cn

Ministry of Foreign Affairs

http://www.fmprc.gov.cn/eng

Information Office of State Council

http://www.scio.gov.cn

News Agencies

Xinhua News Agency
http://www.chinaview.cn
China News Agency
http://www.chinanews.com

TV

CCTV
http://english.cctv.com
CCTV Olympic
http://intl.2008.cctv.com

Broadcast

China Radio International
http://english.cri.cn

External Publicity

China International Publishing Group
http://www.cipg.org.cn
China International Communication Center
http://www.cicc.org.cn
China Internet Information Center
http://www.china.org.cn
China Development Gateway
http://en.chinagate.com.cn

Newspapers

People's Daily
http://english.peopledaily.com.cn
China Daily
http://chinadaily.com.cn

Magazines

Beijing Review
http://www.bjreview.com.cn
China Today
http://www.chinatoday.com.cn
China Pictorial
http://www.rmhb.com.cn/chpic/htdocs/english/

Women of China
http://www.womenofchina.com.cn

Books

Foreign Languages Press
http://www.flp.com.cn
New World Press
http://www.nwp.com.cn
Sinolingua
http://www.sinolingua.com.cn
Morning Glory Press
http://210.72.20.211:3042/main/
Dolphin Books
http://www.dolphin-books.com.cn
China Pictorial Publishing House
http://www.zghbcbs.com
New Star Press
http://www.newstarpress.com
China Intercontinental Press
http://www.cicc.org.cn

Travel Agencies

China International Travel Service Head Office
http://www.cits.cn

China Travel Service Head Office
http://www.ctsho.com
China Youth Travel Service Tours Holding Co., Ltd
http://www.cytsonline.com
China Comfort Travel Co., Ltd
http://www.cct.cn
CITIC Travel Co., Ltd
http://www.travel.citic.com
China Women Travel Service
http://www.cwts.com.cn
China Peace International Tourism Co., Ltd
http://www.hply.com

International Publication Distribution

China International Book Trading Corporation
http://www.cibtc.com.cn/gtweb/new_enhome.do

图书在版编目（CIP）数据

中国2008：英文／钟欣编著. - 北京：外文出版社，2008
ISBN 978-7-119-05207-6
Ⅰ.中…Ⅱ.钟…Ⅲ.中国－概况－2008－英文 Ⅳ.K92
中国版本图书馆CIP数据核字(2008)第048896号

总 设 计：李 萌
协　　调：林希鹤
文本主笔：崔黎丽
文字编辑：王传民　刘 超　韦黎明　吴乃陶
资料收集：李 宁　薛 芊　孔 璞
责任编辑：余冰清
图片编辑：徐 讯　薛 芊　孔 璞
图表编辑：郝胜龙　林希鹤　王振红　孙志鹏
英文翻译：李 洋　严 晶　曲 磊　王 琴　周晓刚　李 磊
　　　　　韩清月　冯 鑫
英文审定：May Yee　王明杰
篆　　刻：骆芃芃
图片提供：新华社图片社　视觉中国　人民画报社　法新社　东方IC
　　　　　兰佩瑾　徐 讯　孙树明　黑 眼　孙伟忠　焦永普
　　　　　华锦州　孙海波
文字与图片终定：徐明强
地图制作：北京好山河文化发展有限公司
审 图 号：GS(2008)866号
设计制作：北京大盟文化艺术有限公司
印刷监制：冯 浩

中国2008

钟　欣编

*

©外文出版社
外文出版社出版
（中国北京百万庄大街24号）
邮政编码100037
北京华联印刷有限公司印刷
中国国际图书贸易总公司发行
（中国北京车公庄西路35号）
北京邮政信箱第399号　邮政编码100044
2008年（20开）第1版
2008年第1版第1次印刷
（英）
ISBN 978-7-119-05207-6
09900 （精）
17-E-6803P